D0247090

Inclusion and Diversity in the Early Years

A practical resource to support inclusive practice in early years settings

by Anne Rodgers and Dr. Elaine Wilmot

Contents

Acknowledgement

Thanks to all the settings used as examples of good practice in this book, including Pembury House and Woodlands House.

Published by Practical Pre-School Books, A Division of MA Education Ltd,
St Jude's Church, Dulwich Road, Herne Hill, London, SE24 0PB.

Tel: 020 7738 5454.

www.practicalpreschoolbooks.com

© MA Education Ltd 2011

Front cover (clockwise): © iStockphoto.com/digitalskillet, © iStockphoto.com/tirc83, © iStockphoto.com/quavondo, © iStockphoto.com/Tomasz Markowski, © iStockphoto.com/Kim Gunkel, © iStockphoto.com/Danish Khan

All photos © MA Education Ltd. 2011, with the exception of p.8 and p.35 © Elaine Wilmot; p.21, p.25, p.40 (left-hand picture), p.42, p.47 © Anne Rodgers; p.5 (left-hand picture) © iStockphoto.com/eyenigelen; p.6 MARY EVANS PICTURE LIBRARY; p.11 (Louise Batalla Duran)/Alamy; p.19 © iStockphoto.com/ktaylorg; p.37 (Kathy deWitt)/Alamy. All photos © MA Education Ltd. 2011 taken by Ben Suri, with the exception of p.13 (left-hand picture), p.14 (right-hand picture), p.28 (left-hand picture), p.53 and p.54 taken by Lucie Carlier.

ISBN 978-1-907241-21-5

Early Childhood Essentials

An introduction to inclusion and diversity

This book has been written for early years practitioners looking to focus on issues surrounding inclusion and diversity within their practice. It is important to focus on what inclusion and diversity really means when working with young children, and its importance in truly understanding the nature of children's differences, similarities, and their development when being cared for in the early years setting. It is vital to meet the individual and diverse needs of all children and to help them reach their full potential.

The Early Learning Goals (QCA, 2000) in England state that children should:

- Understand that people have different needs, views, cultures and beliefs which need to be treated with respect

- Understand that they can expect others to treat their needs, views, cultures and beliefs with respect

- Begin to know about their own cultures and beliefs and those of other people

- Have a developing respect for their own cultures and beliefs and those of other people

Furthermore the *Learning for All: Standards for Racial Equality in Schools* document (CRE 2000) states that effective provision will enable children:

- To achieve their full potential and that expectations are high

- To have access to and make full use of the facilities and resources

- To be prepared for life in a diverse and multi ethnic society

- Be in an environment that has a positive ethos on diversity

Inclusion and diversity is an integral part of effective provision and this book sets out to promote best practice through planning and resourcing early years provision, as well as show how others have achieved this. This book is divided into five chapters as follows.

Chapter one looks at what inclusion and diversity means and why it matters. It asks the reader to consider how inclusive their setting is and also looks at the history of inclusion and considers children with English as a second language. It also considers children with special educational needs, the stereotypes and assumptions made and cultural diversity.

Chapter two will look at the inclusion of children with special educational needs with regards to the requirements of legislation and then will give some information about a range of special needs, with reference to where further information can be sourced.

Chapter three will look at the Early Years Foundation Stage (2008) and what this means when considering inclusion and diversity within the four themes of the curriculum. It also considers Ofsted requirements and legislation in the UK, as well as the rights of children.

Chapter four looks at why working with parents is so important and focuses on establishing relationships with them. It gives ideas for ways to engage parents within the setting and how to continue relationships with them and looks at what may go wrong. This chapter also looks at family learning and inclusive practice.

In chapter five we look at the role of the adult in promoting inclusion and diversity, as well as that of the learning environment. The chapter covers how to promote positive self-esteem and plan effectively to ensure that children's diverse individual needs are met. Examples are given from other practitioners, and next steps and further possibilities explored.

Chapter six looks at leadership and reflective practice and how practitioners can lead by example. This chapter contains a section on selecting staff, monitoring and evaluation.

Chapter 1

What does inclusion and diversity mean and why does it matter?

Inclusion is the process by which we value all individuals, recognising their unique attributes, qualities and ways of being. Central to good inclusive practice are children's rights. The United Nations Convention on the Rights of the Child, (1989) outlines the basic human rights to which children up to the age of eighteen everywhere are entitled: the right to survival; the right to the development of their full physical and mental potential; the right to protection from influences that are harmful to their development; and the right to participation in family, cultural and social life. The Convention protects these rights by setting minimum standards that governments must meet in providing health care, education and legal and social services to children in their countries.

In order to ensure inclusive practice, settings need to develop their ethos, policies and practices to include all learners with the aim of meeting their individual needs.

The Early Years Foundation Stage (DCSF, 2008), which must be complied with in all registered and maintained early years settings in England, states that:

> Providers have a responsibility to ensure positive attitudes to diversity and difference – not only so that every child is included and not disadvantaged, but also so that they learn from the earliest age to value diversity in others and grow up making a positive contribution to society. (DCSF, 2008, p. 9)

It also outlines that:

> All children, irrespective of ethnicity, culture or religion, home language, family background, learning difficulties or disabilities, gender or ability should have the opportunity

Every child has their own specific needs

to experience a challenging and enjoyable programme of learning and development. (DCSF, 2008, p. 10)

There are many definitions of inclusion. The Early Childhood Forum define inclusion as:

> A process of identifying, understanding and breaking down barriers to participation and belonging. (Early Childhood Forum, 2003)

Early years settings must promote an inclusive society in which every person is fully accepted, respected and valued.

This should not be affected by skin colour, disability, social background, gender, religion or belief, or any other factor.

All children should be seen as individuals in terms of their learning and development needs. An inclusive approach to education and care means that difference is recognised and celebrated, and that professionals identify and meet any associated needs through their provision. The task for anyone working with young children and their families is to engage with the physical and emotional needs of young children, bearing in mind the child's racial, religious, cultural background and beliefs.

The inclusive approach is built on respect. It is important that we develop respectful relationships with children and their families because of the potential effects on children's self-image and self-esteem. Showing respect is about demonstrating that you accept the right of others to conduct their lives in ways that reflect their values and traditions, even though these may be different to your own. It requires workers to be knowledgeable and curious, in order to identify and acknowledge difference. Once learning and developmental needs are determined, in conjunction with the child and their family, then outcomes should be agreed, both for the long and short term. The important thing to remember is that every child is an individual and should be treated such. This means that each child has individual: needs; ways of knowing

POINT FOR REFLECTION

It is vital that we do not treat every child the same. They are not the same and by treating them as such, through identical provision we will not be meeting their individual needs.

All children are different. We know that children progress at different levels — some walk early, others are still crawling well beyond the time when their parents expected them to begin walking. Some children are good talkers, others may be late to begin talking. What we must not do is 'label' children and then begin to treat them differently because of that label.

"There is nothing so unequal as the equal treatment of unequals." (Aristotle)

What do you understand by Aristotle's quote?

How do you think about individual needs?

and learning; and ways of responding to the world around them. What it does not mean is treating everyone the same.

When children enter a 'formal' early years setting, a major aspect of our role as practitioners is to ensure that we fully understand each one as an individual — their likes and dislikes, their wants and needs, how they express themselves, their routines — in fact, as much information as we can possibly collect to enable us to welcome each child as an individual. The parents or carers of the child will be the holders of this information.

Why does inclusion and diversity matter?

Inclusion and diversity matters because it is a crucial part of our role as early years' practitioners to secure equality of opportunity for all of the children that we work with. We want every child to be the best that they can be. The Early Years Foundation Stage clearly states that "All children are entitled to enjoy a full life in conditions which will help them take part in society and develop as an individual" (Principles into Practice Card 1.2). One of its commitments is that "No child or family is discriminated against" (Principles into Practice Card 1.2).

Fundamentally, including all children is important because if the child is to develop a healthy understanding of themselves, build an accurate self-image and have robust self-esteem, then they must grow up in an environment where they feel that they 'count'. We know from recent work in neuroscience (Greenfield, 2001; Jensen, 1994) that unless we are in a mentally healthy state, we will be unable to learn. But we also know that in order to form long-lasting, meaningful relationships that we first have to like ourselves.

How can we like ourselves if we are raised in a society where we experience abuse and prejudice because of who we are? Whilst we strive to provide equal opportunities for children, we cannot deny these don't always exist in our society — despite the laws that have been introduced to try and secure it. Social inequalities abound in our society and some children are denied the chances that others will have as a right because of social inequalities, such as stereotyping, prejudice and discrimination.

The Early Years Foundation Stage states that:

Providers have a responsibility to ensure positive attitudes to diversity and difference not only so that every child is

An historical view of the average family

A modern inclusive setting

included and not disadvantaged, but also so that they learn from the earliest age to value diversity in others and grow up making a positive contribution to society. (DCSF, 2008, p.9)

It is our role, as early years practitioners, to try to secure equality of opportunity for all of our children by treating them as individuals.

History of inclusion and diversity

There have been huge changes in society in the last 40 years. We live and work as part of an increasingly diverse population in terms of ethnicity, culture, religion and beliefs. Laws and attitudes have also shifted in that time. For example, in 1968 it was legal to refuse housing, employment and public services to people because of their ethnic background. Our notions on the meaning of the family has shifted over the years too. In the 1970s one child in twelve lived with a single parent, usually because of the a spouse, today it is one in four. Births outside marriage have increased from 8% to 46% in the same period. Social attitudes to sexual orientation have also changed — until 1967 gay men in Britain were imprisoned for sodomy.

It was not so long ago that the 'average' family consisted of a mother, father and supposedly 2.4 children. Today families come in all shapes and sizes, with the increase in divorce

and remarriage, cohabitation and same-sex marriages. In 2006 there were 17.1 million families in the UK — up from 16.5 million in 1996. Most were still headed by a married couple (71%), although the proportion of families made up of cohabiting couples had increased to 14%, from 9% ten years earlier. Although two children remains the most common family size, the average number of children per family in the UK has dropped — from 2.0 in 1971 to 1.8 in 2007.

The way we view children with disabilities has also shifted over the last 50 years. In the 1970s, the 'medical model' was widespread, which ascribed difficulties and disabilities as inherent in the individual. This model views education as a 'cure' or 'therapy' that has the power to minimise or even eradicate the symptoms of a disability. Children were usually admitted to specialist provision or were transferred from mainstream schools to specialist provision as soon as their 'defects' were diagnosed. This diagnostic process worked on a deficit model which seeks to focus on what a child was not able to do, and take these 'deficits' as the lead in looking for ways to eradicate the symptoms. The medical model of disability views the disabled person as needing to fit in, rather than thinking about how society itself might need to change.

Following the Warnock Report (1978), the medical model came under some criticism in the 1980s for focusing on the disability, rather than on the impact of the educational provision on the child's learning. A more interactive approach was developed

In the 1970s the medical model of disability was widespread

at this time where the child's difficulty was seen to arise from a mismatch between the child's needs and provision, whether organisational or curricular. This resulted in a shift of responsibility from the child (and parents) to the school or organisation. It became the school's duty to provide the necessary support for the child. The buzzword was 'integration', formally introduced by the 1981 Education Act. But integration models still assume that there is something wrong that must be fixed in order to fit the child into the present system, for example, adaptations to buildings or additional resources or support.

The 1989 United Nations Convention on the Rights of the Child spelled out, for the first time, the rights of disabled children to be educated in the mainstream. Article 23 of the Convention calls for a child to be educated in a way that will allow him or her to achieve the 'fullest possible social integration and individual development'. The UN Committee on the Rights of the Child has since interpreted this as a goal for inclusion for all children.

In the early 1990s, this then led to a slightly different perspective called 'inclusion'. In 2000, Tony Booth and Mel Ainscow produced a set of materials called the *Index for Inclusion* to help support the development of inclusive schools. This Index was placed in every school by the British Government.

In 2001, the Department for Education and Skills (DfES) defined an inclusive education service as:

POINT FOR REFLECTION

It is important that you understand the make-up of your local community, otherwise how are you going to be able to target your services and meet local needs?

Your setting might have access to its own database, with information provided directly by service users. Many settings have registration forms that collect data on ethnicity and first language, etc. You will have to be sensitive about the collection of this information. Some parents might find questions about their ethnicity intrusive and they might have concerns about what use will be made of the information. You need to consider, particularly if they are refugees, the kind of regimes from which they have escaped and the impact this has on their thinking about government agencies and people in authority.

As an alternative source of information the local authority may also have data that you can access.

One of the best ways to find out about your locality, is to walk the streets surrounding the setting, so that you can see at first-hand what the housing is like, what nationalities you see, and how many young families you can see. This, of course, will only give you a very generalised picture, but it is a start.

You might want to consider the following questions:

- What have you noticed about the population you serve?

- Have there been recent changes?

- How has this impacted on your practice?

- Inclusion is a process by which schools, local authorities and others develop their cultures, policies and practices to include pupils;

- With the right training, strategies and support, nearly all children with special educational needs can be successfully included in mainstream schools;

- An inclusive education service offers excellence and choice and incorporates the views of parents and children;

- The interests of pupils must be safeguarded;

- Schools, local education authorities and others should actively seek to remove barriers to learning and participation;

- All children should have access to an appropriate education that affords them the opportunity to achieve their personal potential;

- Mainstream education will not always be right for every child all the time. Equally, just because mainstream education may not be right at a particular stage does not prevent the child from being included successfully at a later stage.

Inclusive education implies a radical shift in attitudes from the old 'deficit' model, where the assumption was that the difficulties were in the child, to a 'social' model, where barriers to learning exist in the structures and attitudes of society itself. Inclusive education has come to mean the provision of a framework within which all children, whatever their ability, gender, language, ethnic or cultural origin, can be valued equally, treated with respect and provided with real learning opportunities.

Successful models of inclusion believe that all children are different and all children can learn. There is nothing about a child that needs to be fixed in order for that child to fit into a system. The system, as a whole, is enabled to change in order to meet the individual needs of all learners. In this way the inclusion of pupils with special educational needs (SEN) can lead to overall school improvement, as organisational and curricular arrangements are scrutinised in order to address limitations for SEN pupils.

Children with English as a Second Language (ESL)

There has been an increase in the numbers of children arriving in settings who have English as a second or additional language. In the past this was seen as a 'handicap' for the child, preventing them from accessing the curriculum. Children would certainly not have been encouraged to use their mother tongue in the setting because this would stop them from developing their English. In the past, children with ESL or EAL would mostly have been withdrawn from their classrooms for additional language lessons by a specialist teacher.

In 1985, the Swann report, *Education for All*, concluded that beginnners made better progress if exposed to English through mixing with their peers, and recommended that they should be taught in mainstream classrooms, supported by language specialists. The Commission for Racial Equality (CRE) also raised concerns about the marginalisation of ethnic minority pupils, so withdrawal came to be seen as ethically and methodologically unsound and there was a shift towards all children with English as an Additional Language being included in mainstream lessons.

Children who speak English as a second or additional language will be at many stages of learning English. Some will have been bilingual from birth, because their parents will have talked to them in more than one language. Others will be learning English as a second language. As we know, language is learnt best in context, and combined with plenty of opportunities for practical experience and time to talk to others (Ellis, 1999). When children arrive in your setting who do not speak any English, it is quite normal for them to spend a long time listening and not speaking very much at all. They often understand more than they can say at this early stage. It is helpful to use facial expression, gesture, signing and sometimes pictorial representation to aid their understanding.

We know that children who are fluent speakers in their mother tongue are more likely to pick up English quickly, through immersion and by playing and working alongside other children whose English is more highly developed. We should recognise that children who have this ability to speak more than one language should be praised and encouraged to develop all of their languages alongside each other. Parents also need to know that it is important that they continue to speak to their child in their mother tongue. This will aid children's understanding of difficult concepts and help them to understand nuances of words.

When working with a Bengali-speaking girl, aged five, undertaking practical science work in the water tray, the child was asked by the adult working alongside her to give reasons why the cork floated and the orange sank. She replied: "The cork is light and the orange is dark". She had fully understood that light and dark were opposites, but she hadn't understood that light could have more than one meaning. This was shared with the parent at the end of the day and she was able to continue this discussion with her child at home in Bengali, thus developing the child's understanding of the concepts of heavy and light.

LINKS WITH YOUR PRACTICE

Parents need to know that you are interested in them and their child. After all, they are trusting you with one of the most precious things in their lives; their child. They need to feel accepted for who they are and they need to see that you show them respect.

It might be interesting for you to try to view your centre from the perspective of a parent. Start from the main entrance to your setting and make the journey to where a parent would drop off their child.

- What do they see?

- On a normal day, what would be their experience on arrival?

- Would anyone be there to greet them?

In one setting, staff encouraged the use of mother tongue languages by welcoming each child and family in their mother tongue. One member of staff would stand by the door in the morning, welcoming children and their carer as they arrived with a cheery 'good morning' in their own language. This would be accompanied by a warm and sincere smile. This made everyone feel valued, welcomed and respected for who they were.

- Do you know the languages spoken by the children with whom you work?

- How do you encourage the use of mother tongue in your setting?

- How do you model respect for languages other than English?

There are obviously implications here for staff, but they are not being expected to become fluent in other languages, but to merely learn a few words in the main community languages of their setting, such as hello, welcome, good morning and goodbye. While many settings display a welcome poster in community languages, this does not have the same welcoming impact of a smiling face and a welcome in your own language. This is a small way of demonstrating respect for children and their families, which, as discussed earlier, is an important part of developing inclusive practice.

Provide opportunities for children to hear their mother tongue

Opportunities for learning need to be planned to help children to develop their English. Additional support should be provided wherever possible, but the children should not be withdrawn from 'normal' routines and activities for additional language support. This will only serve to isolate them from their peers and they will miss opportunities to learn alongside others.

There are some key provisions that should be made to support children who are learning English as a second or additional language. These are:

- Providing bilingual support where possible — it is fortuitous if bilingual staff are employed, particularly if they speak the main community languages;

- Display writing and books in the children's home languages as well as English (you will need to ensure that you have resources in all community languages so as not to alienate and offend some groups);

- Provide opportunities for children to hear their mother tongue: have story tapes in languages other than English — if you can't buy these, why not make them yourself;

- Provide a range of opportunities for speaking and listening activities so that children can practise their English with peers and adults;

- Show respect for each child's home language; know what languages they speak and learn a few words yourself, so that you can interact with the child.

Children with additional needs

We have already mentioned that children should be viewed for what they can do — we should be interested in their competencies and strengths, not their difficulties and disabilities. By focusing on the positive, it becomes possible to remove potential barriers to their play and interactions.

But most children, at some time or other in their educational career, will have additional needs. These can be transient and short-term needs, brought about because of a new baby, a death in the family, or an illness, for example. These needs are usually short-lived and with a little additional support the child will overcome them and soon revert back to their old selves. Early years practitioners must never forget that the progress and development of all children is their responsibility.

Early years practitioners do not need to be expert in the diagnosis of children with special educational needs for two reasons: firstly, because diagnosis should be left to medical professionals or educational psychologists and secondly, because they are already specialists in child development and have a deep knowledge and understanding of how young children learn. What you do have to do is to really get to know each child by playing and working alongside them, observing them and noticing how they interact with others and the environment around them. If you have any concerns about an individual child's development, then it is good practice to ask the parents or carers, as early as you can, about whether they have noticed what you have noticed about the child. You need to do this sensitively, because you don't want this to lead to a misunderstanding where trust can be lost forever. Think carefully about the language that you use and plan what you want to say and what you want to find out. Do not use any language that could be construed as confrontational or that might give the impression that you have negative expectations. Acknowledge that the parents are the experts when it comes to their child and that you want to discuss something that you have noticed their child doing in the setting, asking them whether the child behaves like that at home and how they deal with it. You should find that approaching parents in this positive way will further contribute to the building of trusting relationships.

If you get the tone of this meeting right, then the parents will be impressed that you know their child as an individual and that you care enough to make enquiries and it will demonstrate to them that you have the child's best interests at heart.

As previously mentioned, it is the role of the professional to be curious about these needs in order to specify what they are and how they can best be met. It is not about labelling the child and isolating them from opportunities available to everyone else. The role of the professional is always to develop your understanding of the child's needs that leads to action, rather than the process of labelling. You must always consider the needs of the child first and the special need second. It is about asking the questions: "How do we include…?" and "What do I need to do in terms of planning and provision to enable....to participate fully?" Learning activities can be adapted and environments can be changed to facilitate greater participation. Advice can also be sought from the setting's special educational needs co-ordinator (SENCO) on the kind of provision that can be made.

Some children's additional needs will be more long-term and permanent, e.g. a child with a physical disability, a parent who has substance abuse issues, or a child in care. Further details on different types of special educational needs, can be found in chapter two.

Cultural diversity, stereotypes and assumptions

Our settings are becoming more diverse in terms of population served and our provision and practice is expected to be more inclusive. But this does not mean that we will not come across people who make assumptions about and stereotype others, either through ignorance or lack of knowledge.

It is likely that you will come across some parents who hold racist views and do not want their children speaking any languages other than English. They will object to you teaching songs in other languages and putting up signs around your setting reflecting community languages spoken. It is important that you explain to these parents the importance of respecting everyone, and accepting them for who they are.

It is a good idea to get your parents to know each other, because often these attitudes are borne out of ignorance.

Once they get to know people from other cultures, they will find that there are more similarities than differences. Early years settings can play a huge part in developing social cohesion, through holding multicultural events, and sharing food, music and culture with each other. It is also a good idea to adopt a buddy system for the parents — so that those parents who are more confident can support those who are less so, particularly if they share the same language.

Of course, there will always be some parents that will persist with their racist attitudes, and it could be that they will have to be issued with a formal warning and maybe even banned from the premises.

Assumptions about gender differences

Society is full of assumptions about gender differences, such as boys wear blue, girls wear pink, boys should be tough, girls should be pretty and big boys should definitely not cry. In some cultures and families this is particularly key to how they think about child rearing. Some dads don't like to see their sons dressing up and playing with dolls, seeing this as 'soft'. They want their boys to be 'real boys', playing football and getting engaged in rough and tumble activities. These parents need to be encouraged to see that it is not effeminate for their sons to be playing with dolls, and that it is in fact a good way for young boys to explore and experiment with emotional engagement.

We need to be careful about the language that we choose to use so that we don't reinforce these stereotypes and assumptions.

A note on 'political correctness'

There has been a lot in the media in the last few years about being politically correct so as not to offend particular groups, e.g. banning Christmas in favour of a winter festival so as not to offend other faiths and religions, not being able to sing *Baa, Baa, Black Sheep* for fear of offending black people and not sharing stories or rhymes with young Muslim children that include pigs because the Qur'an forbids Muslims from eating pork. These media stories tend to be sensationalised and have done little to improve relationships between cultures in our society. There is often no need to make these changes to our practice: but once again, if you are unsure then consult the people you wish to avoid offending.

We need to be more aware of the language that we choose to use, particularly in terms of gender specific language such as fireman or firewoman rather than firefighter. These gender specific terms draw attention to the sex of the person in the position, rather than the role they play.

There needs to be a balance here and common sense should be brought to bear. Most people will not be offended by the celebration of Christmas or the singing of traditional nursery rhymes. What is important is that they are part of a rich and varied approach, so that many different festivals and cultures will be celebrated across the year, particularly those represented by the community.

LINKS WITH YOUR PRACTICE

Every setting must have a designated SENCO (Special Needs Co-ordinator). The SENCO can provide advice and guidance on the provision that needs to be made for children with additional needs. The SENCO's role is to:

- Advise and support other practitioners

- Ensure liaison with parents and other professionals

- Ensure that appropriate Individual Education Plans are in place

- Ensure that relevant information about individual children is kept up-to-date

- Take the lead in assessing a child's particular strengths and areas for further development

- Plan future support for the child

- Monitor and reviews any action taken

- Make sure that appropriate records are kept

Some questions for you to consider:

- Who is responsible for special educational needs co-ordination in your setting?

- How is your SENCO enabled to support other colleagues?

- Can parents seek support and advice from your SENCO?

Case study: getting parents to mount displays

An early years practitioner wanted to mount a display to celebrate Eid, but was uncertain what she could display without causing offence to anyone. She decided that she would ask one of the parents who was Muslim, with whom she had a particularly good relationship, and seek advice from her about what would be appropriate. The parent volunteered to come into the nursery at the end of a day and help the practitioner mount the display, and she brought artefacts and books from her home to put on display. The parent was very proud of the display that she had helped to create and was keen to show it off to other parents. This led to other parents asking if they could provide similar support when it came to the time for their own religious festivals. The impact was not only that some very high-quality displays were produced, but more importantly there was also a knock-on effect in terms of community cohesion. Parents began to show a very keen interest in each other's religions and customs and began to notice the similarities in the way that they celebrated major festivals. There was a marked improvement in the respect shown for other people's cultures.

There were also positive impacts on the children of these parent-led displays. They were very keen to show their friends

Images of how festivals are celebrated in other countries invite interest from children and parents alike

and the staff the artefacts from their home — providing opportunities for conversation and questioning. This link between home and school also impacted positively on the self-esteem of these children. More ideas for working in partnership with parents can be found in chapter four.

KEY POINTS WHAT DOES INCLUSION AND DIVERSITY MEAN AND WHY DOES IT MATTER

- Every early years setting has a legal duty to ensure positive attitudes and difference, to promote equality of opportunity and to value diversity in others.

- Society has changed over time and laws have been modified to reflect the changing population and shifting attitudes to difference.

- The approach in your setting to inclusion and diversity should be based on respect for the individual. Everyone should be valued for who they are and for their unique contribution.

- Children should not be labelled: this prevents you from seeing the child behind the additional need. You should always begin by considering the individual needs of the child and what they can do, building on their strengths and interests.

- Stereotypes and assumptions are unhelpful and these will need to be challenged.

- If you are at all unsure about how your community will react to things you have planned, why not ask them. You will truly demonstrate your respect by consulting the people you wish to avoid offending.

Chapter 2

Including children with special educational needs (SEN)

Defining special educational needs

The definition of Special Educational Needs according to the Education Act 1996, Section 312 is:

A child has special educational needs if he or she has a learning difficulty which calls for special educational provision to be made for him or her.

A child has a learning difficulty if he or she:

a) Has a significantly greater difficulty in learning than the majority of children of the same age; or

b) Has a disability which prevents or hinders them from making use of educational facilities of a kind generally provided for children of the same age in schools within the area of the local education authority.

c) Is under five and falls within the definition at a) or b) above, or would do if special educational provision were not made for the child.

A child must not be regarded as having a learning difficulty solely because the language or medium of communication of the home is different from the language in which he or she is, or will be taught (The Education Act 1996, Section 312).

Where a professional or a parent has a concern about a child, then the setting can instigate Early Years Action. The revised SEN Code of Practice (DfEE, 2000, p.20) suggests that the triggers for intervention through Early Years Action could be a practitioner's concern about a child who, despite receiving appropriate early education experiences:

- Makes little or no progress even when teaching approaches are particularly targeted to improve the child's identified area of weakness;

- Continues working at levels significantly below those expected for children of a similar age in certain areas;

- Presents persistent emotional and/or behavioural difficulties, which are not ameliorated by the behaviour management techniques usually employed in the setting;

- Has sensory or physical problems, and continues to make little or no progress despite the provision of personal aids and equipment;

- Has communication and/or interaction difficulties, and requires specific individual interventions in order to access learning.

Special educational needs provision

Special educational provision means:

a) For a child over two, educational provision which is additional to, or otherwise different from, the educational provision made generally for children of the child's age in maintained schools, other than special schools, in the area

The SENCO and staff should gather information from parents

Invite parents to contribute to their child's learning journey

b) For a child under two, educational provision of any kind

When it has been agreed between the parents and the professionals that the child needs additional support, the Special Educational Needs Coordiantor (SENCO) should be involved. The SENCO and practitioners will then:

- Gather up-to-date information from parents, acknowledging their concerns and gaining consent, where necessary

- Collect evidence through observations and records kept by practitioners

- Gain information from other professionals who may be involved

This information should then be used to support effective planning, based on the individual needs of the child. Strategies should be identified that will support the progress of the child and these should be written into an Individual Education Plan (IEP). The IEP should be reviewed regularly and parents should be involved in these reviews. Outcomes from the review should be agreed by all and recorded with new targets set.

For most children, the additional planning and support provided through an IEP will be enough to enable them to make satisfactory progress.

What do you need to include in an IEP?

1. The nature of the child's difficulties

2. Three or four targets to be achieved in a given time

3. Action:

   - The special educational provision
   - Staff involved, including frequency of support
   - Specific programmes/activities/materials/equipment (included in the curriculum planning)

4. Help from parents at home

5. Any pastoral care or medical requirements

6. Monitoring and assessment arrangements

7. Review arrangements and date

If progress continues to be minimal or the child makes no progress at all, then Early Years Action can be taken a step further with Early Years Action Plus. At this stage, external support services can be called in. Support and advice can be sought from other agencies, such as speech and language therapists, occupational therapists, child psychologists, etc. and specialist strategies can be agreed by all involved, including the parents. The situation must continue to be monitored and regularly reviewed. In a minority of cases, it may be necessary to proceed to the process of statutory assessment. This is when the setting, external professionals and parents ask the local authority to undertake an assessment of the child's special educational needs. A form requesting statutory assessment will need to be completed and it is suggested that all IEPs and evidence of their implementation and outcomes should be attached to this form, so that the local authority has evidence of everything that has been tried to date. It would also help if there were copies of any external reports, such as those from the paediatrician, health visitor, speech and language therapist, etc., and any written views of the parents.

Since 1981, local authorities have had a duty to provide a statement for a child who is thought to have special educational needs (Education Act, 1981). The authority should:

- Assess the child's special educational needs

- Issue a statement which sets out the child's specific learning needs

- Identify the provision required to meet these needs and what the authority will do.

The statutory assessment must follow strict time guidelines, taking no longer than six months, unless there are exceptional circumstances. The case will be considered by a special needs panel. The statutory assessment may or may not lead to a statement of special educational needs. If it is decided that a statement of special educational needs is required, then it will include:

- What the child's special needs are

- What provision is to be made – this would include any specific resources that are to be provided, including any additional hours of support

- How the needs will be monitored

- Where the child should be placed

It is the responsibility of the local authority to name the setting which the child should attend, taking account of the parents' views. It then becomes the responsibility of the named setting to plan and provide for the child's needs and monitor their progress. The statement must be regularly reviewed – on a six monthly basis – to monitor whether the child's needs are being met. The review is led by the SENCO and invitations to attend should be sent to all professionals involved, as well as the child's parents or carers. All professionals involved should be asked to provide a written

Pictures or signs can aid communication

Your observations should inform future planning

report, if they feel it is appropriate. Following the review meeting, information should be collated into a special review form and sent to the local authority and all others involved in the review. This form asks if the child still needs a statement, whether any changes in provision are suggested and includes targets that the child should be working towards before the time of the next review.

Statutory SEN requirements throughout the UK

SEN in Wales

The SEN Code of Practice for Wales (2001) adopts the same working practices as England, explained in this section. Further information can be found at: <http://wales.gov.uk/topics/educationandskills/publications/guidance/specialeduneedscop/?lang=en>.

SEN in Scotland

The Education (Additional Support for Learning) (Scotland) Act 2004 came into force in 2005 and was amended in 2009. This law sets out how children should be helped to get the right support to become successful learners and explains how parents can make sure this happens. Further information can be found at: <http://www.scotland.gov.uk/Publications/2004/02/19009/33932>.

In Scotland, a national programme called 'Getting it right for every child' (GIRFEC) aims to improve outcomes for all children and young people. It promotes a shared approach that:

- builds solutions with and around children and families

- enables children to get the help they need when they need it

- supports a positive shift in culture, systems and practice

- involves working together to make things better

The GIRFEC method supports three initiatives to help children's wellbeing and learning – Equally Well, The Early Years Framework, and Achieving our Potential (for more information on these see the Scottish Government website <www.scotland.gov.uk/gettingitright>.

SEN in Northern Ireland

The law dealing with Special Education in Northern Ireland is contained in The Education (Northern Ireland) Order 1996 as amended by The Special Educational Needs and Disability (Northern Ireland) Order 2005 (SENDO). As a result of SENDO, the Department of Education provides guidance to schools in the form of a Code of Practice on the Identification and Assessment of Special Educational Needs and also a Supplement to the Code of Practice (2005).

There are three stages to the Code of Practice.

- Stage one: concerns are shared with the parents and information is gathered in order to try to meet the additional needs.

- Stage two: the member of staff responsible for special educational needs will talk to the parent and together they will draw up an education plan.

- Stage three: the setting will look for additional support from external agencies. A new education plan will be drawn up which reflects the expert guidance received.

If the child's needs cannot be met, then statutory assessment can be pursued through the Education and Library Board.

Further information can be found at: <http://www.deni.gov.uk/index/7-special_educational_needs_pg/special_needs-codes_of_practice_pg.htm>.

Different types of special educational needs

As early years professionals, whilst we don't have to be experts in special needs, we need to have a basic understanding of the range and type of special educational needs that we may encounter in our work with young children. Special educational needs are generally separated into the following five broad types: developmental delay; a disability or health problem; a speech or language disorder; emotional and/or behavioural difficulties; a learning difficulty such as dyslexia.

The table on pages 17-19 details the five broad types of special educational needs, how to recognise them, the type of support you can provide and where to seek additional information. It is important to reiterate at this point that each child must be considered individually and individual provision should be made for their specific needs, as demonstrated in the following example.

Example: Welcoming a child with SEN

Provision was made to meet the specific physical and educational needs of this child

When a parent approached the headteacher, asking for a place for her child in the nursery class, it was the beginning of a long and sometimes difficult journey for the school and the family. The child in question was a girl, aged four, who was wheelchair-bound due to cerebral palsy. She also had speech and language difficulties. The parents were very keen on their daughter attending a mainstream school, even though the local authority had offered them a place at a very successful special school.

The headteacher, instead of making a unilateral decision, involved the nursery staff in the discussions with the parents, so that issues could be openly discussed and everyone's questions and concerns could be addressed. The staff discussed their needs in terms of the layout of the nursery, so that room could be made for wheelchair access and they were open to working alongside physiotherapists, speech and language therapists and occupational therapists in order to develop their own knowledge and skills.

Agreement was made between the school, the parents and the local authority so that the school could be named on the statement of special educational need for the child.

The parents were encouraged to work alongside the nursery staff for the first week, to enable them to learn how to work with the child. She settled into the nursery very well and staff quickly learned not to be afraid of hurting her when they had to lift her from her chair to the floor, where she could shuffle around on her bottom. The other children loved to play alongside her and would volunteer to push her chair around the garden. Communication was supported through the use of Makaton sign language, which the staff and children learned quickly with the support of the speech and language therapist. Nursery staff learned the necessary physical exercises that needed to be done every day by working alongside the physiotherapist.

The child was enabled to participate in every activity that the other children were engaged in because the staff were very creative about finding solutions to enable this to happen.

The inclusion of this child was very successful because of the joint working between staff, parents and other professionals. Everyone working with her was determined that she would have a positive educational experience.

Table 1: How to support children with different types of SEN

Type of SEN	How to recognise SEN	How to support the child	Sources of further information & support
DEVELOPMENTAL DELAY			
Developmental delay	Is the child at least a year behind what you would expect for a child of that age? In all areas or does s/he have areas of strength?	Additional time to complete tasks Specifically designed activities to meet their needs: ● Learning aids ● Physical therapy ● Occupational therapy ● Speech and language therapy	Contact a Family: www.cafamily.org.uk
DISABILITY OR HEALTH PROBLEMS			
Hearing Impairment	Have the parents mentioned any concerns about the child's hearing? Have you noticed that the child does not always respond when you are speaking to them?	Ensure the child can see your face when you are communicating with them Use pictures or signs to aid communication Encourage children to express themselves verbally	British Deaf Association: www.bda.org.uk National Deaf Children's Society: www.ndcs.org.uk Royal National Institute of Deaf People: www.rnid.org.uk
Visual Impairment	Have the parents mentioned concerns about the child's sight? Does the child screw up their eyes or tilt their head to try to see more clearly?	Ensure that the child always wears their glasses and that these are clean Use enlarged print Enlarge icons on the computer Ensure good lighting — not too bright or too dim	LOOK UK: www.look-uk.org.uk National Blind Children's Society: www.nbcs.org.uk Royal National Institute for the Blind: www.rnib.org.uk
Physical Disabilities	Does the child have difficulty in managing their own basic needs unassisted, e.g. feed themselves, dress themselves, manage the toilet themselves? Is the child able to join in all activities with other children?	Encourage the child to make use of any additional aids that have been provided Physical therapy or other therapies — work alongside experts to learn correct techniques	Association for Spina Bifida and Hydrocephalus: www.asbah.org Association of Wheelchair Children: www.wheelchairchildren.org.uk British Council of Disabled People: www.bcodp.org.uk Council for Disabled Children: www.ncb.org.uk/cdc Whizz-Kidz: www.whizz-kidz.org.uk
SPECIFIC MEDICAL CONDITIONS Most of these condition will have been diagnosed by medical experts prior to the child attending your setting so we have only included how to recognise them for those that you may encounter undiagnosed.			
Asperger's Syndrome or Autism	Does the child have difficulty with social communication, social interaction and/or difficulty with imagination?	Keep instructions short and simple Give the child time to process the instructions Support with visual clues	Oasis: www.oasis.co.uk/aspergers-children The Asperger's Society: www.aspergerssociety.org

Type of SEN	How to recognise SEN	How to support the child	Sources of further information & support
Asthma	Does the child wheeze when breathing? Do they suffer from shortage of breath and coughing?	Ensure the child uses their inhalers to control their asthma	Asthma UK www.asthma.org.uk
Brittle Bones	Physical discomfort and recurring fractures	Be vigilant in terms of recognising when the child is suffering discomfort	Brittle Bone Society: www.brittlebone.org
Cerebral Palsy	Difficulties with movement, posture and co-ordination	Physical therapy, occupational therapy or speech therapy may help the child	4MyChild: www.cerebralpalsy.org SCOPE: www.scope.org.uk
Coeliac Disease	Recurring diarrhoea and signs of malnutrition	This can be managed with a gluten-free diet	Coeliac UK: www.coeliac.org.uk
Cystic Fibrosis	Recurring chest and respiratory infections	Daily physiotherapy and breathing exercises	Cystic Fibrosis Trust: www.cftrust.org.uk
Diabetes	The child urinates frequently and is abnormally thirsty	Controlled with diet control and insulin injections	Diabetes UK: www.diabetes.org.uk
Down's Syndrome	Flat face with an upward slant to the eye, short neck, and abnormally shaped ears Deep crease in the palm of the hand and white spots on the iris of the eye Poor muscle tone, loose ligaments and small hands and feet	Keep instructions short and simple Give the child time to process the instructions Support with visual clues Encourage the child to be independent	Down's Syndrome Association: www.downs-syndrome.org.uk
Epilepsy	Recurring seizures	Staff should be trained in how to respond to a child having a seizure	Epilepsy Action: www.epilepsy.org.uk
HIV or AIDS	Severe bouts of childhood infections	Staff should be trained on the implications of working with a child with HIV or AIDS	AIDS Education and Research Trust: www.avert.org
Muscular Dystrophy	The child may stumble, waddle, have difficulty going up stairs, and toe walk	Physical aids Physical therapy	Muscular Dystrophy Campaign: www.muscular-dystrophy.org

SPEECH OR LANGUAGE DISORDERS

Type of SEN	How to recognise SEN	How to support the child	Sources of further information & support
Speech Disorder — a problem with the production of sounds, e.g. stuttering Language disorder — a difficulty understanding words or putting words together to communicate ideas	Can the child make themselves understood? Does the child readily converse with others? How does the child make their needs known? Do they use speech or gesture?	Show extra patience and sensitivity when listening to the child Always make good eye contact when communicating with the child Provide additional time for them to say what they need to say – never speak for them Provide additional opportunities for them to communicate with you Specialist speech therapy	AFASIC: www.afasic.org.uk British Stammering Association: www.stammering.com Cleft Lip and Palate Association: www.clapa.com I CAN: www.ican.org.uk Makaton: www.makaton.org

Type of SEN	How to recognise SEN	How to support the child	Sources of further information & support
EMOTIONAL AND/OR BEHAVIOURAL DIFFICULTIES			
Emotional difficulties/ Behavioural difficulties	Is the child particularly quiet or withdrawn, suffering with nightmares, bedwetting, withdrawal, low self-esteem, or difficulties forming relationships with other children or adults Is the child's behaviour challenging in your setting and at home? Does the child respond to routines?	Clear boundaries and expectations of their behaviour Highly structured environment Professionals who remain calm when working with these children Show them techniques to manage their emotions and/or behaviour	Hyperactive Children's Support Group" www.hacsg.org.uk
SPECIFIC LEARNING DIFFICULTIES			
Dyslexia	Does the child have difficulty putting together sequences, e.g. coloured beads, days of the week, numbers or even getting dressed?	Use multi-sensory approaches to learning Seek advice on specialist games for use with dyslexic children	The British Dyslexia Association: www.bdadyslexia.org.uk
Dyspraxia	Poor fine and/or gross motor skills Bumps into things or falls over a lot Messy eater Left or right handedness not established	Keep instructions short and simple Give the child time to process the instructions Support with visual clues	Dyspraxia Foundation: www.dyspraxiafoundation.org.uk

KEY POINTS IN INCLUDING CHILDREN WITH SPECIAL EDUCATIONAL NEEDS

- Special educational needs have been defined in legislation (Education Act, 1996, Section 312).

- The SEN Code of Practice (DfEE, 2000) sets out guidance about the provision that should be made for children with special educational needs.

- There are five broad types of special educational needs:

  - Developmental delay
  - A disability or health problem
  - A speech or language disorder
  - Emotional and/or behavioural difficulties
  - A learning difficulty such as dyslexia

- Every setting must have a SENCO

- Whilst we have provided websites where you can access further information, you should always ask the parents first for information about their child's needs.

- Provision for special educational needs can take many forms, for example, learning aids, specific activities or therapies or just additional time to complete tasks.

- There is no one solution that will fit every child who presents with a particular need — each child must be considered individually and individual provision needs to be made for their specific needs.

Chapter 3

Legislation and policy

This chapter will look at the Early Years Foundation Stage (2008) and what this means when considering inclusion and diversity within the four themes of the framework. The chapter will then look at the Ofsted requirements and legislation in England and approach the subject of children's rights. All of the acts, policies and frameworks included in this chapter give the statutory position of frameworks for England in place in July 2011 which affect early years provision. They all include guidance which shapes early years provision based on the principles of inclusive practice and the respect of a diverse society.

Early Years Foundation Stage (EYFS)

There are four themes of the Early Years Foundation Stage framework. These are:

- A Unique Child

- Positive Relationships

- Enabling Environments

- Learning and Development

Each of these themes are enabled by an inclusive provision, and it is important to consider them when providing opportunities for all children, especially those with additional needs.

A key concept in these themes is the idea of 'a unique child', which recognises every child as a competent learner from birth who can be resilient, capable, confident and self-assured. It also goes further to say that every family that attends the setting is unique, and should therefore be included regardless of colour, race, religion, ability or social class. The Department for Children, Schools and Families (DCSF) recommend that settings where possible hold festivals and celebrations to represent the diverse background of the families within the setting and should be valued as a learning opportunity.

Another key strand of the EYFS is that of respect, which runs through the theme of positive relationships. This theme stresses the importance of respecting each other and working in partnership with parents and carers.

Office for standards in education (Ofsted) recommendations

The EYFS clearly states that "Providers must promote equality of opportunity and anti-discriminatory practice and must ensure that every child is included and not disadvantaged because of ethnicity, culture or religion, home language, family background, learning difficulties or disabilities, gender or ability". (DCSF, 2008, p. 37)

Settings must take all reasonable steps to ensure children with disabilities can have access to the premises. In meeting this statement, all activities should be available to all children and adapted where necessary taking into consideration their age and stage of development, gender, religion and culture. Children with medical and dietary needs need to be considered and allowances made for their care. Families choosing not to participate in activities have the right to do so; this may be due to cultural or religious reasons. Also, parents may choose to follow a particular routine for their child and this should be respected as much as possible.

It is a requirement for each setting to submit a Self-Evaluation Form (SEF) prior to an Ofsted inspection. Table 2 provides examples of evidence that you can include in your SEF (according to the Ofsted 2009 Self-Evaluation Form for Early Years Settings) to demonstrate your inclusive practice.

Example: Celebrating Chinese New Year

Making a dragon to use as a display model

Using the dragon to inspire dance

A day nursery manager was conscious that the setting did not plan enough for various festivals throughout the year, and asked her staff in the pre-school room to consider what might be relevant to children in the nursery. As there was a Chinese family in attendance the staff chose to celebrate Chinese New Year. When asked for their input the family were happy to contribute by collecting money bags for the children, as well as menus and samples of Chinese writing. Using these resources the staff created a Chinese restaurant to encourage pretend play in the home corner. Staff gathered large boxes and plastic cups and made a Chinese dragon out of papier mâché, which was used in dancing, before being hung from the ceiling as a display. The children thoroughly enjoyed art activities such as flag making and using chopsticks with noodles in the messy play area.

Interest tables and displays which reflected the festivities helped to cement the learning and allowed parents to see what their children had been up to in the setting. This encouraged further discussion amongst parents, who wanted to get involved and brought items in from home that they thought we might like to use.

Initially, some members of staff were reluctant to explore other festivals and celebrations but the manager pointed out that the families in attendance that were not from the area would benefit greatly from such focus, as could the rest of the families who attended the setting. After the Chinese New Year celebrations the staff could see for themselves how interesting it was to learn and teach children about celebrations which were new to both them, and many of the children. This celebration of other cultures and festivals enabled both staff and children to gain an appreciation of other cultures and beliefs, and meant that the minority of children in this setting who came from other cultural backgrounds gained a sense of belonging and acceptance by feeling valued and included. Activities were adapted for children with additional needs so that they too could join in, for example a child in a wheelchair particularly wanted to dance under the dragon, so another child helped push her along while she held the dragon's head and led the dance. Most of the staff felt that it made the planning easier to have a particular focus in mind and they saw how easily these topics fit into the Early Learning Goals and requirements of the EYFS for learning as well as individual children's needs.

Table 2: How to demonstrate your setting's inclusion policy using Ofsted's self-evaluation form

Area of Self Evaluation Form	Detail requested by the Self Evaluation Form	Evidence that could be included	Advice to be found in this book
Part A: Setting details and views of those who use the setting	Describe the main characteristics of your setting and the culture and backgrounds of the children who attend, including those who have learning difficulties and/or disabilities, or speak	Setting data on ethnicity, languages spoken, additional educational needs as well as local data on local population such as levels of poverty, etc.	Chapter 1
Section 1: Your setting	English as an additional language.		
Section 2: Views of those who use your setting	Ofsted want to know about the views of the children and their parents or carers who attend your setting.	Questionnaires and surveys feedback from parents and other users of services. Feedback from children.	Chapter 3
Part B: The quality and standards of the early years provision	Ofsted want to know how your provision promotes children's welfare and their learning and development.	Plans for individual children, based on information from observation and assessment	Chapter 4
Section 3: Quality of the provision	You need to make sure that your provision meets all the welfare and learning and development requirements set out in the Early Years Foundation Stage framework.	Evidence of how you involve parents and carers as partners and other agencies and providers in children's learning and development	Chapter 3
Section 4: Outcomes for children	This section is linked to the five Every Child Matters (ECM) outcomes ● Achieve and enjoy ● Feel safe ● Adopt healthy lifestyles ● Make a positive contribution ● Develop skills for the future	Evidence of monitoring outcomes for children, e.g. records, learning profiles, assessments, transition documentation.	Chapter 4
Section 5: The leadership and management of the early years provision	How inclusive and welcoming is your service? Consider how effectively you promote equality of opportunity and tackling unlawful discrimination. Consider how well you work in partnership with others, such as other settings children may attend, or another professional who is working with a child. Try to explain the impact of the partnership working. Consider how well you communicate and engage with parents and carers and take account of their views.	Policies on admissions, inclusion, special educational needs, challenging behaviour. Monitoring of racist incidents, other incidents and complaints. Minutes of management committee/ governing body/advisory board/parents' forum. Minutes of any inter-agency/ multi-disciplinary meetings. Staff training records. Newsletters and other communications to parents.	Chapter 4
Section 6: The overall effectiveness of the early years provision	This section provides an opportunity for you to explain the effectiveness of the early years provision in terms of meeting individual needs of all the children who attend and how well you promote the five Every Child Matters outcomes. The central question is 'What is it like for a child here?'	Outline the process of evaluating outcomes for children, identifying areas for improvement, any consultations with parents and/or children and any resulting changes	

Further consideration of how to prepare for an Ofsted inspection is included in chapter six.

Legislation and inclusion

Many laws have been passed regarding childcare and education over the centuries and some of the most influential ones of recent years are listed below. It is important for early years professionals to gain an understanding as to why we do what we do and how we came to be able to offer the kind of child care and education that is on offer today. Legislation is ever-changing and practitioners need to keep themselves updated with the changes in the law to ensure that they are operating legally within their settings.

Legal requirements for inclusion and diversity

The following list includes Acts of Parliament which have passed regarding the care of children and education which are more closely associated with inclusion and diversity and have this as their underpinning theme. Practitioners need to be aware of current affairs and political reform to understand the impact on their role and act upon any new recommendations.

Education Act 1993

This Act made important and far-reaching changes to the educational system in that it put in place a new system for primary and secondary schools. It meant that parents had more say in the education of their child, the schools themselves more autonomy over how they are run, and the central government more say in how education was delivered.

This Act incorporated all previous Education Acts since 1944. Part four of this Act included the main elements of the 1993 Education Act in relation to SEN. It gave parents increased rights to appeal and also set a limit of 26 weeks to complete the legal process for identifying and assessing special needs. This Act is still current, but has been amended by the Special Educational Needs and Disability Act 2001 to give parents and children stronger rights to be included in mainstream education.

Disability Discrimination Act 1995

This legislation promoted civil rights for disabled people and protects them from discrimination. It stipulated that all disabled people had the right to employment, a good education, have access to goods and facilities, and be able to live independently in adapted accommodation. Public bodies had to promote equality of opportunity regardless of ability.

Human Rights Act 1998

The fundamental rights that all persons have as defined by the Human Rights Act are:

- the right to life

- freedom from torture and degrading treatment

- freedom from slavery and forced labour

- the right to liberty

- the right to a fair trial

- the right not to be punished for something that wasn't a crime when you did it

- the right to respect for private and family life

- freedom of thought, conscience and religion, and freedom to express your beliefs

- freedom of expression

- freedom of assembly and association

- the right to marry and to start a family

- the right not to be discriminated against in respect of these rights and freedoms

- the right to peaceful enjoyment of your property

- the right to an education

- the right to participate in free elections

- the right not to be subjected to the death penalty

If any of these rights are breached, you have a right to be protected by law, even if the breach was committed by someone in authority, such as, for example, a police officer. This Act came into effect in October 2000 and incorporates provisions from the European Convention on Human Rights. It has wide-ranging implications for many areas of people's lives, as all government initiatives and decisions must be interpreted in line with the agreed articles and the protocols of the convention. These include the right to education and the prohibition of discrimination.

The main principles: there are three main rights which the Convention says must be considered whenever a decision is made about children or action is taken which affects them:

- Non discrimination. All rights apply to all children regardless of race, sex, religion, language, disability or family background.

- Best interests. When decisions are made about children, they should always consider the best interests of the particular child.

- The child's opinion. Children have a right to say what they think about anything which affects them. They should be listened to carefully and have their views taken into account.

SEN Code of Practice (2011)

This Act replaced the 1994 Special Needs Code of Practice, which stipulated that all children have the right to mainstream education, regardless of their ability. The 2011 Act went further by stating that the local education authority, schools and early years settings, health and social services have to comply with the Code of Practice to ensure that the needs of children are being met through an integrated and gradual approach. The 2011 Code put stronger emphasis on working with parents, children and other outside agencies. It meant that children with special needs could be integrated into mainstream school. This also meant that any professional working with the child and their family could request the right to an assessment being made on the child.

Children Act 2004

This law was passed as a result of the inquiry into the death of Victoria Climbie at the hands of her carers. Lord Laming published a report showing that this child had 12 missed opportunities, when professionals could have worked together to save her from abuse. This Act ensured that every child could be electronically tracked via medical, health and educational routes, such a tragedy that this could never happen again. It also introduced the core requirements of Every Child Matters. The Act stipulated that there should be a Children's Commissioner for England, as well as statutory local safeguarding children boards to protect children.

The five required outcomes of Every Child Matters which apply to all children are as follows:

- Stay safe

- Be healthy

- Achieve economic well-being

- Make a positive contribution

- Enjoy and achieve

This Act surpasses the Children Act of 1989, which stipulated that children are kept safe and well and to offer help and support to families by providing services that met their child's individual needs. The 2004 Act went further by ensuring that any of the agencies directly in contact with a child are accountable for their safety. It also placed greater responsibility on local authorities to promote educational achievement for looked after children.

Ten-Year Childcare Strategy: choice for parents, the best start for children (2004)

This policy would see that the Government would provide high-quality integrated early education and childcare services; and give parents more choice in how they balance their working and home lives in providing flexible childcare services that met their individual needs. The government also set out plans for a children's centre in each community offering help and support and advice, enable access to benefits and support services, and to increase the free early education from 12.5 hours a week to 15 hours a week for three and four year olds. Out-of-school care was increased for children aged between three and 14- and parents consulted on planning and delivery of early years' services.

Childcare Act 2006

The Childcare Act has four parts: duties on local authorities in England (part one), duties on local authorities in Wales (part two), regulation and inspection arrangements for childcare providers in England (part three) and general provisions (part four). Key provisions are as follows.

- Sections 1-5 require local authorities and their NHS and Jobcentre Plus partners to work together to improve the outcomes of all children up to five and reduce inequalities between them, by ensuring early childhood services are integrated to maximise access and benefits to families — underpinning a Sure Start Children's Centre for every community.

- Sections 6, 8-11, 13 require local authorities to secure sufficient childcare for working parents that meets the needs of the community in general and in particular those families on lower incomes and those with disabled children.

Example: Assisting all children's language development

Looking at keyring pictures from the Chatter Box

A day nursery has a range of children at different stages in their language development. There are groups of children with communication difficulties, and children with English as an additional language. In order to ensure all these children are fully supported in the setting the setting manager developed both the resources available and the knowledge of the staff team. The setting employs team members who are bilingual so as to ensure as many children as possible can communicate in their home language if they want to. The setting also uses Makaton signs for children with communication difficulties.

In order to promote more communication in the setting the manager created a 'Chatter Box'. This box featured a set of laminated cards, each of which had either pictures, Makaton signs, or single words. Some of the cards were put onto keyrings in order to make them more transportable. This resource encouraged communication between children, as well as offered opportunities for children to develop their knowledge and understanding of both the different items on the cards, as well as how other children communicated. Shortly after this, the nursery was inspected by Ofsted, and the statement below reflects the positive report on the setting's inclusive attitude to early language development.

"Makaton signing is used for key vocabulary throughout the setting and assists all children's development in communication, language and literacy. The setting provides very good support for a number of children with speech and language difficulties and physical disabilities. Children with English as an additional language are very well supported with a bilingual member of staff and books of key words in both languages. Key workers take excellent responsibility for individual needs and specific programmes to assist children's physical and speech development."

The children gained a lot from using the 'Chatter Box' in ways to support their individual stage of language development. Staff observed children's play with this resource in order to identify next steps in Communication, Language and Literacy development. What is more the 'Chatter Box' pictures and cards could be changed regularly to offer new ideas and interests.

A key target of The Children's Plan is to improve child health

- Section 7 re-enacts the duty for local authorities to secure a free minimum amount of early learning and care for all three and four year olds whose parents want it.

- Section 12 extends the existing duty to provide information to parents, to ensure parents and prospective parents can access the full range of information they may need for their children right through to their 20th birthday. Local authorities will be required to ensure that this service is available to all parents and that it is pro-active in reaching those parents who might otherwise have difficulty accessing the information service.

- Sections 39-48 makes the Early Years Foundation Stage the legal framework for all children from birth to age five.

The Children's Plan (2007)
This Act set out the plan to build a brighter future for children and their families by 2020. Its aims are:

- To secure the wellbeing and health of children and young people

- To safeguard the young and vulnerable

- For individual progress to achieve world-class standards, and close the gap in educational achievement for disadvantaged children

- For system reform to achieve world-class standards

- Ensure that young people are participating and achieving their potential to 18 and beyond

- Keep children and young people on the path to success

- To set out a vision for 21st century children's services

The Children's Plan also set out what could and should be achieved by 2020. These goals included the support of all children through transitions in their lives, and that every child would be ready for school and developing well across the Early Years Foundation Stage Profile by the age of five years. Child poverty should be halved by 2010 and eradicated by 2020. Children's health should be improved, and childhood obesity levels reduced. All of these aspirations would be under review and revised accordingly.

Statutory Framework for the Early Years Foundation Stage (2007)
The Early Years Foundation Stage (EYFS) is a framework which was launched in 2007 and came into force in September 2008. It is the new regulatory and quality framework for the provision of learning, development and care for children aged 0-5 years. The Childcare Act 2006 provides the legal framework for the Early Years Foundation Stage (EYFS). For more on the EYFS and inclusion and diversity see page 20 of this book.

The Common Assessment Framework for children and young people (2007)
The Common Assessment Framework (CAF) helps to deliver integrated services to children and young people. It is a

standardised approach to assessing the needs of children and young people and how best to meet their additional needs. It promotes early identification taking into account the role of the parents, carers and environmental factors which may affect them. All local authorities are expected to implement this process via a lead professional — someone who will coordinate on behalf of the child — and the sharing of information between other professionals working with the child and their family.

Equality Act 2010

In October 2010, the Equality Act became law, replacing the Race Relations Act (1976) and Disability Discrimination Act (1995). The section on school provision stipulates that no school can unlawfully discriminate against any of the following protected characteristics:

- Disability

- Gender reassignment

- Pregnancy and maternity

- Race

- Religion or belief

- Sex

- Sexual orientation

Age and being married or in a civil partnership are not protected characteristics for the school's provisions.

Private early years providers (such as private day nurseries, childminders, accredited childminder networks, pre-schools, playgroups and Sure Start Children's Centres) which provide childcare to pre-school children come under the service provider provisions which are explained in separate guidance. <http://www.equalityhumanrights.com/advice-and-guidance/information-for-service-providers/>.

United Nations Convention on the Rights of the Child (UNCRC)

The United Nations (UN) is a group of 193 countries. They work together on a number of issues which affect everyone in the world. They created a list of rights that every child should have called the United Nations Convention on the Rights of the Child (UNCRC). The UNCRC is a list of 42 promises made by governments from almost all countries (except USA and Somalia) in the UN to children and young people, including the right to education, equal treatment and the right to an opinion. All governments who have signed the UNCRC are supposed to work to make it part of their law. The UK agreed to obey the Convention on the Rights of the Child on 16th December 1991. The following articles are most relevant to the themes of inclusion and diversity: 2, 23, 29, 30 and 31.

Further information can be sought at the following web address: <www.unicef.org.uk>.

KEY POINTS IN LEGISLATION AND POLICY

- Think about the EYFS and its links to inclusion and disability, and relate this to your own setting. How do you provide for children with additional needs and celebrate their cultures?

- How do you prepare for Ofsted inspections with regard to inclusive practice? The SEF form offers a great way to promote your ideas on inclusion and diversity and provide evidence. Keep a file of evidence for each area to provide proof that you are meeting requirements.

- The legal requirements of each setting and legislation and policies need to be clearly thought out and reflect best practice. How often are your policies updated? Are parents included in the process?

- Understanding the rights of the child and how it impacts on the way we provide for them.

- Make other staff aware of the rights of the child through staff meetings and information leaflets.

Chapter 4

Working with parents and carers

We have included a chapter on working with parents and carers because they are central to their children's lives; they are the child's key educator, know their children better than anyone else does; and they care very deeply about their children. Parents need to feel included and it is part of the role of the early years professionals to ensure that parents' diverse needs are met in order that they can continue to support their children's learning and development.

Parents play a crucial role in the education of their children. There is a wealth of research (Evangelou and Sylva, 2003; DCSF, 2008) that shows that children do better when:

- There is a close working partnership between home, early years settings and school

- Information about children's learning is shared between everyone involved in the child's successful development

- Parents show a keen interest in their children's education and make learning a part of everyday life

- Children are actively involved in making decisions about their own learning

The DCSF report *The Impact of Parental Involvement on Children's Education* (2008, p.2) found that 'parental involvement in children's education from an early age has a significant effect on educational achievement, and continues to do so into adolescence and adulthood.' The report goes on to say that it is the quality of time spent with children that contributes most to outcomes and the attitudes and aspirations of parents predict later educational achievement. It recognises that the level of parental involvement varies among parents, with mothers, parents of young children, black or black British parents, and parents of children with a statement of special educational need being more

Establish regular communication with parents

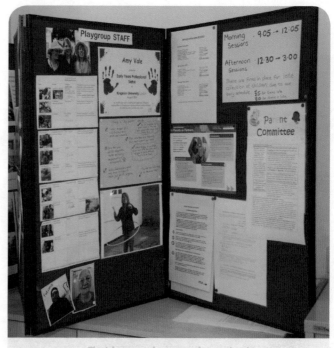

First impressions are important

likely than average to be involved in their child's education. This is significantin terms of our thinking about inclusion and diversity because there may be groups of parents, e.g. fathers, who will need to be encouraged to become more involved with their children's learning.

For these reasons, working in partnership with parents becomes central to the future educational success of children. In order to work in partnership with parents, you need to be aware of what parents want for their children, as well as their expectations of you and your setting. You will need to build trusting relationships by listening to them, respecting their way of life and valuing their knowledge about their children.

Current context

The family unit has changed drastically over the last 20 years and can be made up of a number of different families living in the same household. The diversity of the family must be considered before deciding how best to incorporate working together. The family unit may look like this:

- Extended family with generations of the same family all living together

- Nuclear family (married couples with children)

- Reconstituted families with step parents and siblings

- Single parents

- Children living with just their grandparents

- Shared households with multiple families who are not necessarily related to each other

- Cohabiting parents with children

- Gay or lesbian parents

When getting to know our children we need to understand what kind of background they come from, their cultural needs, and type of family, their housing needs and any other issues relating to home as this will have an effect on their child's learning and development. For example, if a child is living in a multi-storey block of flats they may well need space to run around and get involved in physical activities at the setting, as there may be a lack of opportunity at home.

We not only need to work closely with the children in our care, but also their families, parents and carers. It is essential to build a good relationship with the child's parents, so that the best interests of the child can be met in a way that is suitable to the needs of the parents and carers in a mutually agreed and effective way. This ensures continuity of care and respect for each other's role in the life of the child.

Parents are sometimes returning to work out of necessity rather than choice, and so may feel terribly guilty at having to leave their child for such long periods of time with a stranger. These parents may feel resentful of the bond that the child has with their key person, and the developmental milestones that they are missing out on, and it is important to establish good communication as well as a relationship of trust with parents or carers.

Establishing a relationship with parents

Communication

This means the clear and effective flow of information between parents and practitioners. Parents need to be kept informed and should be consulted with at every stage of their child's development and it is vital to build strong links between the parents and the setting to ensure that the child is at the centre of all that is being done.

Trust

Parents need to feel that they can trust the people working with their child and they need to be reassured that there are adequate safety and security measures in place to ensure that their child is safe, secure and well-looked-after. The only way to build this trust is for you and your staff team to earn it. You need to demonstrate to parents that you are trustworthy and that you maintain high standards in terms of providing the best possible care and learning experiences for their children. You can demonstrate this by showing that you meet statutory requirements and that you have considered all aspects of your provision by not only writing but implementing policies and procedures. It is good practice to have a noticeboard or file where current policies and procedures can be displayed for parents to refer to. In this way, they can see for themselves what is entailed in each policy. Being able to access this information for themselves will engender trust because parents will see that you have nothing to hide. You could also encourage them to make comments or suggestions to improve your policy and procedures by providing a whiteboard or Post-it notes for parents' use.

What parents want

In our experience, we have never met a parent who doesn't want the best for their child. Some parents do have difficulty in knowing what is best or how to provide what is in the best interests of their child but fundamentally, we all want the same for our children. We want them to be happy, content with who they are, and successful in whatever future they choose to pursue.

POINT FOR REFLECTION

What you can do

All of the families that attend the setting should be treated fairly and with respect regardless of the ethnic origin, cultural beliefs, ability, colour, economic class or gender. Some families may not have English as their first language, which may cause communication difficulties, but translators and interpreters can be sourced from the local community to help to explain the information you need to pass on and to make sure that it is understood. Leaflets and pamphlets can be sourced in different languages which may help if they are displayed appropriately for adults to access easily.

Displays and posters should reflect the cultural diversity within the setting and promote feelings of acceptance and welcome all families. Ideally, there should be a collaborative communication between parents and staff to gain the necessary information about the children and so that the parent can have a say in their child's care and education.

The child's learning journey or profile book should be accessible at all times and be contributed to by the parents and the staff in the setting.

The policies and procedures of the setting should be made known to the parents so that they get a fuller picture of what their child is doing and why staff have to perform certain procedures.

Some questions for you to consider:

- How inclusive do you think your setting is for parents?

- How do you know how inclusive it is? What is your evidence?

Although as parents we all want the same thing, every family is unique and it is important that we spend time finding out about our families so that we can best support the children in our care. Obviously, the people who hold the information are the parents and we need to think carefully about how we access it. We don't want to appear nosey and intrusive — it is not about prying into their home circumstances, but developing an understanding about how they work with their child at home, so as to build on this learning most appropriately within the setting.

Home visits

Some settings now arrange for a home visit to the child and their family before starting, this can mean that you get an insight into the home circumstances of the family and meet with them in a less formal way and discuss the child's needs and routines. The child will get to meet a member of staff in their own environment and so this will help to settle the child in the setting as the adult will be familiar to them. You can begin to establish the relationship with the child and parents in their home setting where they may feel more comfortable to talk to you.

These visits should never be undertaken alone for the health and safety of the workers involved, so planning in a time for them to take place is essential. It is good practice to home visit in pairs, where one person can concentrate on developing a relationship with the child whilst the other concentrates their attention on the parents.

Home visits facilitate getting to know children and families

A lot of settings have devised their own home/setting documentation or 'getting to know you' forms to aid them in collecting the kind of information that will be useful to them. There are generally two kinds of information — the formal information needed on the child's record and the kind of informal information that will aid the settling in of the child to the setting. The formal information that you will require will include:

- The name of the child on their birth certificate

- What the child prefers to be called

- Names of the parents

- Names and dates of birth of siblings

- Addresses of the child (and the parents if different)

- Who should collect the child from the setting

- Emergency contact details

- Languages spoken by the child

- Religion

- Medical needs, including allergies

- Dietary requirements

The kind of informal information that you might find useful in settling the child might include:

- The child's favourite toy or activities

- Whether the child is left or right handed

- What comforts the child when they are upset

- How the child asks for the toilet

- Whether the child is happy to play whilst their parents are in another room

- Whether the child is used to leaving the parents to visit relatives or friends

- Whether the child plays with other children on a regular basis

LINKS WITH YOUR PRACTICE

First impressions count and parents need to feel welcomed from the moment that they set foot inside the setting as well as in the way that they are shown around and spoken to.

When being spoken to on the telephone parents need to have their queries answered as quickly as possible and they need to feel listened to. Customer service is a vital part of ensuring that the parents are happy with the service that is provided and that they feel listened to and respected. This will help parents to gain confidence in the provision and recommend for others to send their children there.

Provide parents with additional information where possible and pass on your knowledge and experience when required. The professional knowledge and expertise of the staff is invaluable to parents, but they must not feel patronised. Each parent is the child's first and foremost educator and knows more about their child than the practitioner does. If we work together with them the child will have the best possible care and education.

Consider the impression that your setting makes on new parents. What impression does their first experience of your setting give them?

- Whether the child has the opportunity to play outside

- Whether the child likes looking at books or listening to stories — what is their favourite story?

- Whether the child has any favourite songs or rhymes

- Whether the child has favourite television programmes

- Whether the child is good at sharing toys with other children

- Whether the child has any particular fears or dislikes

Of course you need to be careful how you go about asking these questions — nobody wants to feel that they are being interrogated and that judgements are being made about the level of ability of their child. You will need to engage the parents in conversation rather than fire questions at them and reassure them that you only want to know so that you ensure a smooth transition between home and setting. You want the child to settle quickly and the more you know about the child's needs and wants, the more appropriate you can make your provision.

Most parents are reassured that the setting they are entrusting their child to cares enough to find out about their needs and wants before starting.

Other things you can do to ensure a happy home visit include taking along some materials with which to engage the child. A bag which holds paper, crayons, a jigsaw puzzle, a soft toy and some small world play items will enable you to talk to the child about their likes and dislikes. You could also encourage them

to draw a picture for you that you could then take back to your setting to frame and display on the wall with the child's name on in time for the day that they are due to start with you. This will make a good link between home and your setting.

Another top tip is to take a digital camera with you and take a photograph of the child with their parent(s) in the home setting. This can then be printed out and used on the child's personal space within your setting, e.g. their drawer, coat-peg or locker. It can also be included in the child's learning profile.

Although these are quite small things to us, they mean a lot to the child and their parents. They reinforce that we really care about them and that we respect them for who they are.

If parents do not wish for you to attend a home visit then this should be respected.

Setting visits

The first visit to the setting is a crucial one for parents as first impressions do count. Let them have a look around all of the rooms if they wish and offer to show them planning charts, menus, photographs of other children — with their parents' permission — enjoying activities and experiences. Show them the daily routine aspects of daycare and what you propose to do with their child in their absence. Discuss with them their child's needs and routine and how you can meet this within the daily routine of the setting. Enquire about any allergies or medical or dietary requirements and take an interest in their child's likes and dislikes. Reassure parents that you conform to Ofsted inspections, have trained and qualified staff and allay any initial fears about separation by telling them of your settling-in policy and any other policies and procedures. Invite them to look at your Ofsted report and let them know how much you value the place you work in and the achievements that you are most proud of. This gives the parent the feeling that you actually love your job and that this is the place that their child will be best placed to come to. Give them an opportunity to ask questions and to go away and reflect on what they have seen and call you if they need to ask further questions. The parent is investing in you as a professional to make a difference for their child and to take the best possible care of them so it is worthwhile giving them accurate and professional feedback in answer to those questions.

You need to bear in mind that you can never change a first impression and that parents do talk to each other and any bad experiences that they have had in your setting will soon be

LINKS WITH YOUR PRACTICE

Let all parents know that all staff are Criminal Records Bureau (CRB) checked and that they are qualified and to what level. This can be done efficiently and effectively by having a noticeboard with staff photographs displayed along with their role and level of qualification, either in a central location (for all staff) or at the entrance to each room (for those staff members working in there).

Explain to parents what is involved in the care and education of children in the setting and point out what happens and why. Talking to parents and explaining issues and procedures will help towards building up trust and mutual respect. Encourage parents to stay for periods of time in the setting to see how the routine works and what you provide for meals and snacks. Show them the planning cycles and learning journeys of other children who attend so that they may form an opinion of how things are done and what it is that they think their child will enjoy. Get to know the child's routine, ask questions about what it is that the child likes and does not like, do they have any allergies or special toys for comfort that could be taken into the setting to help them and support them when the parent leaves? Some settings have a 'getting to know you' form which the parent will fill out to explain all of these things and then it can be kept and referred to by all staff if necessary. There is more about this later on page 33.

How do you establish trusting relationships between staff and parents?

What else could you do?

shared with the parent's family, friends and acquaintances. This can only have a negative impact on your setting, so it is vital that all staff are aware of the importance of their initial contacts with visitors to your setting.

Open days

Each setting should, if possible, schedule an open day to invite prospective new parents into the setting. Activities can be put on for their children, which are age and stage appropriate and meet the needs of the children, while their parents are in discussion with staff that are in attendance. This is a unique way of delivering the message that the setting is at the heart of the community and that it values and respects the families that attend. You can demonstrate that you listen to the needs and requirements of your community by hosting an open day at the weekend when the parents are free to attend. Parents will then be free to wander around the setting with their child and see what is going on, and perhaps book a visit to come back when the setting is fully functioning to decide on whether to send their child there.

Invite other professionals to attend and get in touch with the local school and family services to ask for their support and let the parents see what a good and collaborative working relationship you have together. Even if the parent decides not to send their child to your setting they may well advertise the fact to other parents and through word of mouth the setting gets new customers, so it can be a good opportunity for marketing your services within the local community.

Continuing the relationship with parents

Collecting information

Whilst it is good practice to collect information about the child and their family before they start in your setting, it is even more vital that the flow of information is continued throughout the relationship. This has to be a two-way process between the home and setting.

Parents need to know how important it is to keep you informed of any changes in their circumstances because of the potential impact this can have on the child. Information that parents should be encouraged to share with practitioners including:

- Unexpected changes in lifestyle, routine or family structure

POINT FOR REFLECTION

Transition from home to setting

Home visits can be very important in establishing a positive relationship between the home and your setting. It eases the transition if the child and parent know someone in the setting. We have to remember that for some of our parents, entering your setting will be a big step. They may have had very bad experiences of learning themselves and you don't want these to be reinforced or transferred to the child. Beginning the relationship with the family on their home ground can be a very positive start.

Some questions to consider:

- Does your setting undertake home visits?

- How effective are they at establishing the relationship with children and their parents?

- How is the information collected used within the setting?

- How has this practice impacted on the settling in of the children?

- The child's achievements

- Worries or difficulties

- Illness and immunisation

- Their child's likes and dislikes

- Any change in contact numbers or change of address

- Any change in who will be collecting the child

Parents will need to be reassured that this information will be treated respectfully and not shared more widely than it needs to be. Staff who are working directly with the child will need to be informed, but you will also need to consider who else needs to know.

You will need to think about how you will put systems into place to enable parents to share this valuable information with you in a safe way. One of the best systems is that of key working.

Parent questionnaires

Another good way to ascertain the views of the parents and carers who attend the setting is to hand out questionnaires asking them about their thoughts, and feelings about the setting. These can be rated on a scale of 0-5 off how happy they are with the services provided, with '0' being not happy, and '5' being extremely happy. Questions can be devised depending on what it is that you wish to know and categorised accordingly. You may decide to ask open questions and leave spaces for answers or have a yes/no answer type of question. Some settings will send these out once a year and some once a term.

You might also consider the use of an evaluation exercise after special events or sessions too. This will provide you with invaluable feedback on how successful the event has been and might give you suggestions on how to improve it in the future. Feedback from parents can then be used to inform future planning of developments or projects. In order to be inclusive, this does not necessarily always have to be a written exercise — you could ask for pictorial evaluations sometimes. For example, using digital cameras at an event and asking parents (or children) to take a photograph of something that they have particularly enjoyed or valued will give you a very clear picture of how successful the event has been.

Comments or suggestions boxes or books

It is also a good idea to have a comments and suggestion box or book for parents to make their wishes known. Think about where these are placed. If kept in a place where parents might feel intimidated by staff watching over them whilst they fill it in, then you are not going to get many parents contributing suggestions. Once you have had an anonymous comment or suggestion make it known via the newsletter that you value their opinion and have done the following things as a result. Another way to let parents know that you have listened and taken appropriate action is to put your responses on a whiteboard to keep parents regularly updated. This will encourage more parents to offer their thoughts and ideas.

Sometimes you will be unable to act positively on the suggestions or comments made by parents. You need to keep them informed as to the reasons why you have been unable to meet their needs on this particular occasion and perhaps offer alternative solutions or ideas.

Sharing information

As well as collecting information from parents, you will want to share information about the work of your setting. There are a number of ways that you can do this, including noticeboards, displays, websites. You might also want to consider more public access to information about your setting through displays in localities used by your families or prospective families such as local clinics, supermarkets, libraries, etc.

Websites

Most settings will have their own website which can be accessed by potential families to the setting as well as existing ones. Offer a variety of suggestions and tips on care and education, provide plans of the routine and age and stage appropriate activities. You can advertise special events and activities to invite new customers in and involve current families. Once again, you will need to consider the design of your site and the information that it includes to ensure that it is as inclusive as possible.

Policies and procedures

It is vital that all parents of the setting are familiar with and know how to access the policies and procedures of the setting. These policies should be freely accessed and available for parents to read and you may even have a system in place whereby parents get to sign to say that they have read them.

Getting parents involved

There are many ways that settings can involve parents in their work. You should never forget that the parents are the first and most important educators of their children, so they should be as involved in their child's learning as they are able. Some parents will be in a position to devote lots of time to supporting their child and others will not. In order to be inclusive in your practice, you will need to be mindful of this when organising opportunities for parents.

You will need to consider the times of day when parents are invited into your setting and the days of the week. You should try to ensure that events are not always scheduled at the same time on the same day, which might make it impossible for some parents to attend because of their personal circumstances.

There are some things that you can do that can include all parents. For example, the use of learning journeys, profile books or home-setting books can be made accessible to all parents.

Make your website interesting, informative and accessible

Encourage parents to spend time in your setting

Home-setting books

For working parents, a home to setting book can be very useful. It can be a way of communicating information to each other about things that have happened at home or in the setting. It need not take a long time to fill in — just quick messages between the key worker and the parent. It can include questions that they have of each other, things that have happened, reminders about things that are needed to be brought in, and a way to share the child's achievements.

Contribution from parents

Parents can contribute to the setting in different ways. They may help with outings and trips, they may get items of need for the setting or be able to provide recyclable materials for projects. They may be able to volunteer some time to work alongside children, sharing their skills and talents or supply unwanted office paper from work for the children to draw on.

You must respect the fact that some parents may be too busy with work commitments to help, but they may be able to help in other ways such as with sponsored events by providing prizes or helping to sell raffle tickets.

However you decide to involve parents, be mindful that you want your practices to be as inclusive as possible — the last thing you want is for certain groups of parents to feel excluded or left out.

Making use of parents' skills

A lot of parents of children in a setting have skills that they would be willing to share with you. Some are good at sewing, some play musical instruments, some may be able to come in and share their passion for a sport, others will be great at telling stories, some like to cook or garden, some have interesting jobs that they could talk to the children about and others may feel able to talk to the children about their religion or culture. By inviting the parents to be part of the children's learning experiences you will enhance the relationship between parents and the setting, and parents will feel more involved and included. The question you need to be considering as a setting is how do we find out what our parents can offer? Getting them to fill in a form can be quite scary for some parents, so it may be best to develop this knowledge over time as the relationship develops. Think about opportunities that can be created for parents to share their skills and then think about which parents you could approach. You will need to make sure that it is not always the same parents afforded these opportunities because that would not be inclusive. If you find that it is always the same parents or groups of parents contributing, try to encourage others by personal invitation and offer to support them. One of the reasons that they may not feel able to contribute may be due to low self-esteem or fear of not being considered able or knowledgeable. Always remember to thank parents for their contribution too, perhaps with a certificate or card of appreciation from the children.

Example: Parents as volunteers

Volunteer parents can provide valuable extra skills which enrich what you offer children

The leader of an early years setting was very keen to involve parents as volunteers for several reasons:

- To provide extra pairs of hands in the setting

- To utilise the skills and talents of parents in order to enrich the 'curriculum' and provide opportunities for parents to get a better understanding of what early learning involved

- To provide opportunities for parents to develop their confidence as a way of getting them back into work

She spoke to the staff to ensure that they would be supportive of the policy to include parents as volunteers, enabling them to voice their concerns and this led to the development of a volunteer policy. The leader then planned a training programme for the volunteers and shared this with the staff team so that they could make suggestions as to what they felt needed to be included in the training.

The programme was promoted to parents via a newsletter, with a tear-off strip to complete, which asked for their name, their child's name and class, and any special skills or talents that they felt would be useful to the setting. Dates were given for the initial training session and parents were asked to sign up.

The first session covered some policy issues such as safeguarding, health and safety, and confidentiality. It also included a brief input from a member of staff on schemas and then parents were encouraged to consider their own child's schemas and share some examples with each other. The group also visited a class and observed the learning before discussing what they had observed, and considering the learning outcomes for some of the activities.

The staff leading the training session treated the parents as co-professionals, encouraging them to share openly any questions that they had. At the end of the training session the parents were presented with a certificate and were asked to complete their Criminal Records Bureau form.

The volunteer programme was very successful and parents became useful colleagues alongside staff who were willing to share their knowledge and expertise.

Volunteer programme

You may want to think about starting a volunteer programme, so that parents can get experience of working in an early years setting with a view to building up their confidence before returning to work. You would obviously need to ensure that safeguarding procedures were in place so that children were always kept safe and so that volunteers would not be compromised. These procedures should include having a member of staff with responsibility for overseeing the work of volunteers, as well as applying good basic practice in terms of allocating volunteers to activities and individuals. Never expect too much of volunteers or see them as a way of ensuring everyday staff-child ratios. Ensure that volunteers are never asked to take on a responsibility that would require them to be on their own with children. Provide some basic information for volunteers — key policies and arrangements for first aid, fire safety and child protection procedures. Ensure risk assessments are in place for the involvement of volunteers and that those working frequently with children do have a CRB check and that the details are recorded for Ofsted inspections. There may be someone in your local authority who can advise you on setting up a volunteer programme.

Outings and trips

Outings to places of interest within the community are a great way to involve parents in that they can help to escort the children with you and maintain the 1:2 ratio required for safety reasons. By involving them they will get a good idea of how the staff organise a group of children and experience for themselves the wonder that the children show when being introduced to new experiences. Visits and outings help to break down barriers between staff and parents as you are sharing a valuable experience with their child and you can both contribute to it in different ways.

Involving parents on outings can break down barriers

The venue for any outing needs careful consideration as it is important to know what the children will be doing and whether it is appropriate for all children. A lot of venues offer free visits for staff who are planning to take groups, so it is worth making a pre-visit so that you can be really well prepared.

It is good practice to ensure that every child is wearing a label with the name and phone number of the setting on it so that, should they get lost, contact can be made quickly and the child can be safely re-united with the group. Never include the name of the child on this label. You could also record any individual requirements of the child on this label, for example, dietary restrictions and allergies.

KEY POINTS IN WORKING WITH PARENTS AND CARERS

- There should be a close working relationship between the parents and the setting. Research (Evangelou and Sylva, 2003; DCSF, 2008) has shown that this impacts positively on the outcomes for children.

- The family unit has changed drastically over the last 20 years. Policies and practice need to reflect your local community.

- There are many strategies used by settings to engage parents — you need to consider which ones are relevant

- First impressions are important and can never be changed. You need to consider your policy on welcoming visitors to your setting, so that everyone is made to feel welcome.

- Home visits can support the transition between home and your setting, for the child and their family. You can begin to establish close working relationships by meeting children and parents in their own surroundings.

Chapter 5

Planning and resourcing

In this chapter we look at planning and resourcing effectively to ensure we are meeting the needs of the children in inclusive ways, using examples from early years settings to show how activities and events can meet children's diverse needs. There are four main areas to consider when deciding what activities to promote with young children. These are:

- The role of the adult

- Learning environments

- Promoting positive self esteem

- Record keeping, planning and assessment

The role of the adult

To find out about the children in our care we usually have a settling in period where we get to know the family and the child and can assess how best to implement the transition from home to the setting so that the family feel comfortable, safe and can trust the key person to care for their child as they would wish. The settling in period is invaluable and each setting should have a settling in policy. This will explain to the parents how their child will be cared for within the nursery. The setting will have a key worker system and each child will have their own special grown up to relate to while their parent or carer is not there. This will help the child to separate from their parent or carer much more easily as they will develop a bond with their key worker. Ideally the room should be laid out in a welcoming fashion that is accessible to all who use it, and staff should be approachable. The routine and way the room is set up should be kept the same during the 'settling in period' as children need a sense of order and a routine can be established, enabling them to explore their surroundings. On settling in, children will become aware of the rules of the nursery and the areas of play and exploration as well as interacting with others, which can be difficult at such a young age.

The key workers role is to encourage the child to mix with other children and to be respectful of each other. By reassuring children who are new to the setting you are helping them to feel a sense of belonging and that they are accepted, when children feel secure and safe they can then begin to explore the environment around them and try new experiences. Children have the right to good quality care and provision and need to have this in order to thrive and become independent. Their feelings must be taken into account and they may need lots of initial support when they make the transition from their home environment to the setting. This time will also give the key worker a chance to learn about the child in his/her care and their families, their likes and dislikes etc., as well as help the child to settle in and integrate themselves into the routine and the setting, and get to know more about each other and their community. The parent is the child's first educator, so building relationships with parents is vital to the overall wellbeing and care of the child. Through the parent you can find out what the child's needs are so that you are better equipped to meet them. Parents and practitioners can learn from each other and should work together for the benefit of the child. Play and the environment are essential to a child's learning. Young children have a right to high quality learning experiences and high quality care. It is the role of the early years practitioner to ensure that the child is involved in the planning and organization of activities and, they can readily access resources.

Learning environments

Children are most responsive in the formative years (birth to five), this is when we need to build confidence, self-esteem and knowledge to trigger active learning. Play is the most effective method of learning for children and the practitioner is the most valuable resource as their knowledge and understanding of the child and their development and needs denotes which activities are provided and how. The environment should be safe, warm and nurturing in order for children to be able to feel comfortable, confident and have a sense of belonging to enable them to discover and learn. Play should be a pleasurable, enjoyable and fun experience for children reflecting on each child's ability, culture, gender and beliefs and in accordance with the Foundation Stage framework.

The following areas of play all reflect different aspects of the learning environment, and how each can be used to be truly inclusive of all children in the setting. It is important to consider a range of cultures and abilities especially in settings where families are mainly all English and white.

The open-ended nature of art supports inclusive learning

Creative and imaginative play

This type of play offers rich opportunities for children to express themselves freely and use their imagination to make and do things by themselves. Children should be offered the possibility to interpret the available resources in their own way, with or without an end product. The following section identifies key areas of creative development and how to ensure the resources provided promote an inclusive learning environment.

Painting and craft

Using paint brushes of various sizes, their fingers, utensils or printing objects, children will enjoy many styles of painting. Brushes and utensils should be adaptable for use by all children in the setting. Skin tone colours of paint, crayons or paper should be used whenever possible so that a child can paint a picture of a member of their family or themselves accurately. Practitioners should remember that it is not the end product that is important but the creative process itself which is beneficial to a child's development. Displaying a child's work helps young children feel valued and encourages a sense of belonging to the setting as well as a sense of pride in their achievements. Try to place work where a child can see and refer to it, rather than at adult-level. Parents often enjoy having pictures and paintings sent home so that they can display them, and this helps develop links with the home and the setting

Example: Making story sacks for young children

Sacks of toys bring stories to life

Incorporate cultural stories into your storytelling

One idea to support children's language development and literacy is to organise a lending library of story books and story sacks which include props for parents to borrow and return. One practitioner did this and reported that the parents thoroughly enjoyed the experience with their children, as they could borrow a variety of books and props they may not otherwise have had access to. The children also enjoyed sharing their news at circle time as to which books they had read at home with their family.

To begin your collection of story sacks start with one story, such as that of *Chicken Licken*. Read the book first of all to decide which props might be needed and start collecting the mentioned animals in a box, bag or sack. For this story you will need a chicken, hen, duck, turkey, goose, and of course a fox. Either plastic or soft toy animals will be fine and can be resourced easily from a toy shop, car boot sales, or charity shops. The local scrap store may have material for sacks or items such as wooden spoons for puppets. As the story is read the props can be taken out of the bag and given to the children to hold and explore.

Song sacks can be made in the same way to stories with a toy representing a song for example:

- Duck — *Five Little Ducks Went Swimming One Day*

- Star — *Twinkle, Twinkle Little Star*

A student from a setting made a song sack at college for *Old McDonald Had a Farm*. She made a sack for the animals by sewing two pieces of cotton together and then sourced some soft animals to go inside it. When she brought the sack into the setting she was pleased at how the children responded to such a simple idea. She said that she sat a small group of children on the floor and they began to sing the song. She let the children each take a turn of choosing an animal from the bag and hold onto it while the song was sung, the children enjoyed the experience and wanted to repeat the song again and again, choosing a different animal each time.

Incorporating cultural stories and songs, and building up a range of these will be interesting for the children and families to gain ideas from. The local library will have a selection of multicultural books, or alternatively the Children's Centre advisory teacher may be able to get some for your setting.

Drama and role play

Many stories can be acted out by children as a means of self expression and of delving into the story. Cultural tales and stories from other countries can be celebrated and brought to life by the children themselves through pretend play. Parents may wish to be involved in providing costumes or painting backgrounds, or have props which can be used to add authenticity. Children can act out different roles from a variety of backgrounds and 'pretend' to be somebody or something else which helps to develop their imaginative skills, and also helps children develop a sense of empathy. Learning to see things from another's point of view is beneficial for children to help develop social skills and an understanding of the needs of others. Drama in particular can be used to help explore a child in the setting's disability or culture. For example, festival stories and songs can be read and acted out, as well as stories regarding disability being explored through the children finding out what it is like to be in a wheelchair or not be able to see or hear.

Dressing up clothes and props need to be gathered and made freely available and accessible to provide for spontaneous play.

Music and movement

Every setting should have a variety of music and musical instruments. These can be representative of music from around the world and include instruments from many countries. This enables children to have a sense of belonging to their culture. Children should be allowed to discover these for themselves and practitioners can invite parents or visitors to play them for them. Perhaps let parents know what plans are in place for coming activities and ask for input and help. Parents may have instruments at home that they could bring in for the children to look at, or costumes and music that they can share with the setting. For example, one parent had a friend who played the sitar and he came to visit the setting to play for the children during Diwali celebrations. Having music from other countries helps a child to have an understanding of the similarities and differences of other cultures and traditions.

Stories and books

Choosing stories and books on a variety of topics within the local community will help develop a child's understanding of the world around them. They will often relate to the characters or the events that occur and this will help discussion, memory, understanding, empathy, sharing feelings and vocabulary. There are many interesting books readily available that include events and festivals, and display children and families of all backgrounds, cultures and religions and abilities. These should be made readily available to all children in the setting and where possible invite families to read them with their children. Making use of the library service in the local community and the children's services will allow settings to have access to bilingual books and books depicting the wider community, with images of children and families from various backgrounds, colours, faiths and abilities.

Home corner

The home corner is an ideal opportunity for child-led activity. By providing materials and props you are setting the scene for children to experiment and use their imagination to act out and create scenarios either from memory, real-life situations or fantasy. For this area it is useful to have various home environment resources including dolls, tea sets, play (or real if replenished regularly) food, cots and dressing up clothes, reflecting the different cultures and backgrounds of the group. These can be simply made and might be a project for the parents to get involved in to contribute to the setting. Children come from all kinds of backgrounds and live in a variety of dwellings. They may live in a flat, a bungalow or house, in temporary accommodation, be a traveller or live in a caravan. Displaying pictures of all of these types of homes will help children understand differences and similarities and also have a sense of self-worth and belonging as they share pictures and stories. For example, one member of staff, with parental permission, visited each child in the setting and took a picture of them outside their home. She then returned with the pictures to the setting and made a display for all of the children to see. The children loved pointing out to each other where they lived and what type of house and garden they had. Obviously, this project only worked as all of the parents agreed, and so no child was left out. Pictures of other dwellings were also displayed to show the children other homes and types of dwellings that families live in around the world. The activity was followed up with the story of *The Three Little Pigs*, as well as other books and small world play which depicted homes and where both animals and people live.

Small world play

Dolls houses and small world items are a great source of imaginative and creative play and can depict people and families from other countries, abilities and backgrounds. Children can act out various scenarios and find out about other cultures and faiths and explore issues affecting them and their own ability and beliefs.

Hat box

Making a hat box and collecting hats from a variety of religions and cultures, countries and job roles will enhance imaginative play and allow children access to explore other cultures and ways of life. A large mirror can be placed alongside the box to allow children to admire themselves in the mirror and see what they might look like as somebody else.

Puppets

Puppets can be made to depict ethnic origin, culture or ability. They are a way of displaying and acting out inclusive situations and exploring feelings and emotions and can be hugely beneficial in the personal, social and emotional skills young children need to develop their own sense of self and how to belong to a group, community and society. Children can make their own puppets from bags, socks or material and decorate with wool, bits of other material or draw on them to take ownership of their own puppet. These can then be used to act out roles and scenarios as they wish.

Cooking

This is an excellent topic to discover a range of food choices and taste recipes from around the world. Again, parents can be encouraged to provide recipes or bring in items for tasting. When celebrating festivals you can use foods from that country for children to sample or help to cook. Find pictures of a range of foods from the different food groups and cut some out, older children may be able to cut these out themselves. Using a paper plate ask each child to stick on pictures of the foods that they like, this is a useful way of introducing the concept of healthy eating and also getting the child to talk about what they like and dislike. Cooking with children is an enjoyable

experience and they can learn more about each other and taste differing foods and recipes from other cultures and countries.

Some simple ideas are:

- Pizzas: you can use crumpets lightly spread with tomato sauce and choose from a selection of vegetables and cheeses to decorate either as 'faces' or just as pizza toppings. These can then be grilled for a few minutes until cooked.

- Face cookies: biscuits can be iced with different coloured icing to represent skin tones and smiley faces put on using sprinkles or sweets

Circle time

Circle time can be a useful way of discussing topics concerning the way families celebrate things and how they dress and what they eat. Each and every one of the children can contribute to discussion and offer ideas for activities and experiences based on their own experiences and of the experiences they are curious about. It is an ideal opportunity to discover children's likes and dislikes, cultures, religions, family types and discover what they know already about who they are.

Dressing up

Dressing up clothes can be either made or bought, and can be a great way of signifying different cultures, religions and

Puppets of the world can help develop a sense of belonging

Making iced biscuits represent different skin tones

festivals. Access can be made for all children to dress up by using different fastenings or making them loose fitting. Children love to pretend to be different and dress in a variety of costumes with many accessories. Allow them to experiment and explore.

Heuristic play

This is a type of play where children discover for themselves through a variety of resources. Look at Elinor Goldshmeid's (2004) research and work on promoting heuristic play and see how she suggests that it is sourced and managed within a setting or the child's own home. The benefits of heuristic play is that children get to discover and find out things for themselves, we plan for experiences to maximise this and offer resources to nurture the children's natural curiosity and their need to explore and experiment while utilising positive play opportunities. Heuristic play materials are often seen as the second stage to treasure baskets and discovery boxes as the children are more inclined to pursue discovery and be mobile enough to select their own pieces rather than the ones placed in front of them. This type of play is generally most beneficial to the 16-36 month-age-group and for use by children with additional needs. By using everyday objects familiar to the children will help them to problem solve and find uses for new found skills such as opening and closing, posting and rolling and transporting. It fits in well with established schemas and provides lots of opportunities for repetition and hand-eye coordination. This in turn promotes child-initiated learning and is the foundation for creative development and imaginative play. The best method of introducing heuristic play within a setting is firstly to ask staff what they think should be collected and what is already available, ensure that they understand what it is you are trying to achieve and why. The staff team needs to be committed towards exploratory play and not feel that it is an enriching experience for the children as well as them. Parents may be able to help with collections and draw string bags or boxes made to keep them in so that there are a variety of different heuristic boxes available to add variety. There should be a clearly defined space available with little else in the room to distract the children when doing heuristic sessions as they will be able to gain the most from the experiences. Think about the time of day that it is to be offered. Are the children going to be tired or hungry if it is too late in the morning? The items are displayed and children invited to choose things to explore and discover. Staff are free to observe the children while they are engrossed in play and make choices for next steps of development. The children can then be involved in the tidying up process and allowed time to re-examine items not yet discovered or presented in a different way. The role of the adult is a secondary one. The bulk of the

POINT FOR REFLECTION

The best resources a setting can have are the adults who provide interesting and exciting activities and experiences for the children who attend. Look at the work of some of the theorists who are primarily concerned with the environment and how children play. In particular McMillan, Steiner, Montessori, Isaacs, Piaget and Vygotsky. How does your setting link with these theorist's beliefs, both indoors and out?

LINKS WITH YOUR PRACTICE

- Who has a say in which resources are used within the setting?

- How are resources sourced and maintained?

- Have you discussed with staff how to make use of available resources to further develop inclusive practice?

POINT FOR REFLECTION

Think about the heuristic play materials that are in the setting. A scrap store is an ideal place to pick up items really cheaply if not for free. Find out if there is one in your area, or if there are shops, factories or workplaces willing to donate items for the children to use. Start collecting things from home, and ask parents to start collecting. Involving others in providing resources for the children should be considered as part of your inclusive practice.

LINKS WITH YOUR PRACTICE

Make up some heuristic sacks from old pillow cases or boxes that contain items from different groups. For example, metal objects, sensory sacks, wooden objects, a seaside them bag, shiny objects or fabrics with different textures. Ensure that they can be accessed by everyone regardless of ability. Think of sensory explorations and how children who have a disability or impairment may use the resources.

Example: Heuristic play with a group of toddlers

Treasure basket play can easily be replicated at home

The manager of a day nursery was interested in developing heuristic play sessions with toddlers aged 15-36 months, so she asked a playworker from the Children's Centre to help them with heuristic play. The playworker came and modelled a heuristic play session with the staff and children and made appointments for some further sessions with different resources. A newsletter was prepared for the parents asking them to bring in various items from home or to start collecting things that the setting required such as boxes and kitchen roll tubes. The playworker returned for the first time with wooden resources, then shiny resources and finally metal resources. She encouraged the staff to sit on the outer perimeters of the room and observe what the children did with the materials on offer. The staff were amazed at the focus and interest the children took in something different being offered to them and by remaining on the outside of their play allowing them to explore for themselves. The staff set about sourcing their own resources for future activities. The manager asked the Children's Centre teacher for some information on schemas that she could use in a meeting with the staff of the setting. Leaflets were made for parents describing what it is that their children were doing and why,

and how this linked to Early Learning Goals and the theory of schemas and early years development. The children all had a lot of fun and staff were able to meet observed next steps in the children's learning and also prepare equipment for later use as a result of these sessions. Some of the parents expressed an interest in the sessions and ask for further information on how to repeat them at home. The staff modelled a session for the parents and showed them age- and stage-appropriate items for the children and also for the children with additional needs. A basket containing cultural cooking equipment and utensils was made for the children, which parents contributed to. The other rooms of the setting containing older and younger children also expressed an interest and decided to make baskets and boxes of heuristic play resources for their children's age groups too. All in all this was an excellent example of how to promote best practice across the setting with regard to children's ages and needs.

The baskets and boxes could be added to and changed regularly to maintain children's interests and also to allow time for collections to grow.

work will have been done in collecting, resourcing and planning a convenient time for play to begin, the rest of the time should be spent in a supervisory role and observing what the children do and how they behave during the session. The adult then discards any broken or damaged items and plans to replace with something else. There is usually a 'Scrap Store' available in most communities where free resources can be collected fora small membership fee, which allows the setting to revisit as often as they wish.

Outdoor environment

Children love to play outdoors, and with a variety of equipment. Giving them opportunities to exercise their muscles, get some fresh air and allow for physical exertion are all essential to the setting's daily routine. Ideally there should be free-flow outdoor and indoor play where the children can have access to both the indoor and outdoor environment at any time.

Assault course

Building or making an assault course will be hugely beneficial for the children in helping them to take risks and exercise muscle groups to help their gross motor development. Make sure that there are plenty of mats laid down in case somebody does fall off the equipment. Try to provide items for young children to crawl through, jump over, walk across and run around. For example: a tunnel can be crawled through which leads on to a bench to walk across and balance on, which then leads on to a hoop to climb through, some wooden steps to climb up and jump off, and some beanbags to throw into a bucket. Children will enjoy the fun tasks that they can do, as they like to master new skills and if praised will want to repeat them. Ensure less able children have alternative routes to follow or make the assault course more user-friendly by using wider equipment or supplying extra adult helpers. Think about the children who will be using it and make it fit their next steps in learning and development.

Race track

Use some chalk to mark out a large 'race track' onto the ground that has an inside line and an outside line. Road signs can be painted up by the children and placed around the track including a zebra crossing. Cars, prams, trucks and bikes or wheelchairs can be ridden on or pushed around the track. This is an excellent activity for a fundraising event as children can be sponsored to go 5 times or so around the track. Everybody can then have a balloon or a medal for taking part and hopefully lots of money will be raised for a special event or new equipment for the setting.

Den building

Dens can be made using simple clotheshorses and sheeting or by tying fabric to a fenced area so that there is a place to hide in. Children should be given the opportunity to build them for themselves with adults offering support or ideas. Boxes and crates can help make seating areas or areas to climb on. It is a good idea to have den building material in moveable parts so that it may change shape or move from one area to another easily.

The seasons provide many activities for young children, and using the outdoors to explore nature and the differences is an excellent activity for young enquiring minds. Gathering leaves, blossom or conkers, making snow balls or snowmen if you are lucky enough to experience a snowfall, watching new shoots appear in the garden, feeding the birds, and having space to run around and expend all of their energy are all vital learning experiences for young children. Be inventive and creative in your choice of activity for them, or better still let them decide how to use the area. The outdoor environment must be made accessible for all children to enjoy whatever the weather. Do take into account that some children may be from other countries where they do not experience four seasons, and may only have a rainy season and a dry season.

Other Ideas

Festivals and celebrations

According to the Early Learning Goals (DCSF, 2008) it states that children should:

- Understand that people have different needs, views, cultures and beliefs which need to be treated with respect

- Understand that they can expect others to treat their needs, views, cultures and beliefs with respect

- Begin to know about their own cultures and beliefs and those of other people

- Have a developing respect for their own cultures and beliefs and those of other people

Therefore, it is important to focus on the children in the setting and celebrate their festivals and events as they arise. *The Learning for All* document (CRE, 2000) states that effective provision will enable children:

- To achieve their full potential and that expectations are high

- To have access to and make full use of the facilities and resources

- To be prepared for life in a diverse and multi-ethnic society

- Be in an environment that has a positive ethos on diversity

To promote good practice in the early years, children must have full access to the educational programme that reflects our diverse communities and different cultures. There may be children with dual nationalities, who speak English as a second language, or who have specific religious or cultural beliefs. It is up to the practitioners to work with the families and carers of these children and find out about the children in their care. Celebrating festivals helps children to rejoice in their differences as well as their similarities, however there may be some families who wish to abstain from inclusion when celebrating festivals other than their own and this must be respected.

These are some of the festivals and celebrations celebrated within early years settings.

January:	New Year
February:	Chinese New Year
	St Valentine's Day
	Pancake Day
March:	St Patrick's Day
	Mother's Day
	Holi
	St Piran's Day
April:	St George's Day
	Easter
May:	May Day
June:	Father's Day
July:	Independence Day
August:	Carnival
September:	Harvest Festival
October:	Halloween
	Ramadan
November:	Diwali
December:	Christmas

There are many more festivals and celebrations than we have selected here and the ones you choose to celebrate should reflect the local area, customs and events, religious backgrounds of families and staff, and the cultural diversity within the setting. It is up to the staff to gain information on how parents and children celebrate

POINT FOR REFLECTION

When thinking about the outdoor environment practitioners need to consider all areas of the EYFS, as the outdoors is such a rich environment to meet these requirements and can be a useful learning opportunity. Many topics can be explored such as minibeasts, gardening, growth and weather. How do you provide opportunities to meet the whole framework whilst meeting children's individual needs?

LINKS WITH YOUR PRACTICE

- Look at the resources in the outdoor environment. What areas of the framework are lacking? Is there sufficient storage for new equipment?

- Do all of the children have full access to the area?

- What additional provision will need to be made for children with physical disabilities?

and ask the families to contribute and share ideas, should they wish to. After this background research has taken place activities can then be planned to maximise learning and enjoyment of these festivities.

Promoting positive self-esteem

In order to develop into confident and capable human beings children need to have a positive self-image and a strong sense of self. Children need to feel valued and important and capable of achieving and tackling new opportunities and challenges. Offering praise and recognition to children when they are achieving and learning makes them wish to repeat the behaviour and gain more praise and recognition. Negative comments and prejudices help lower self-esteem and make children feel unworthy and therefore less likely to achieve their full potential. Practitioners need to value and respect all families who attend the setting and make sure that they are included in all aspects of learning and development. It is vital that young children grow up in a positive, stimulating, challenging, accepting environment regardless of their ability, gender, culture or background. Staff can help children by exploring the differences and similarities of

Example: Investigating different types of homes

Den making with blankets

Den making with netting

One setting decided to investigate with children how people live, and different types of homes by reading stories and doing a display. This activity started with the story of *The Three Little Pigs* and was followed by asking the children what type of home they lived in. A display was made of pictures that the parents brought in of the children in their homes. Other dwellings from around the world were also included in the display. The staff enhanced the learning opportunity by running activities outside which included building the homes of the three little pigs using hay bales from the local farm, sticks collected from a nature walk to the woods, and plastic construction bricks. A father of a child in the setting is a bricklayer and brought in some real bricks to show the children, who marvelled at the weight of the bricks. This interest prompted activities on the concept of heavy and light in other areas of learning. Secondly, the staff built some dens and gave the children opportunities to make their own. Resources were brought in from home, such as fabric, clotheshorses and boxes. The children constructed a variety of dens around the garden using: pop-up tents; swathes of material and netting attached to the fence using pegs; and cardboard boxes. The staff observed the children and were able to make provision for the next steps for children's imaginative play, creative and physical development, and knowledge and understanding of the world.

The children requested the same materials each day that week for their outdoor play and were observed making the same dens or improvising larger or smaller ones. One child was even observed making a ramp for another child's wheelchair to go through the entrance of the den, and explained that "My nanny has one of these at her house". The staff noticed this and discussed with the children at circle time the need to change things if needed so that everyone could be involved. The next step from the observations that the staff had made was to look at homes around the world. Pictures from around the world of other families' homes (sourced from the internet) were shown to children. Some of the children in the setting had been lucky enough to visit places like this to see their extended families who lived in other parts of the world, and so were able to discuss this with the others, and on one occasion bring in pictures of their families' home to show.

the people around them and explaining why these differences and similarities can occur. Children are keen observers and are constantly trying to make sense of the world around them. Therefore open and honest explanations help them to form opinions, instead of forming stereotypes and prejudices.

Record keeping, planning and assessment

In order to plan activities for young children we firstly need to understand: their needs; likes and dislikes; their stage of development; and the resources that are available. All children are individuals with unique range of abilities, and respond differently to stimuli and situations. Observations allow practitioners to gain an insight into providing engaging activities and supporting children's next steps for development. Observations should be made on a daily basis as part of the child's routine, by the child's key worker or others working closely with them. They can then be analysed to highlight the child's achievements or areas for development and support within the framework of the Early Years Foundation Stage. By regularly looking at and noting down what a child is doing we can get to know the child better and develop a positive relationship with them and their parents, further develop our own understanding of child development and plan the next steps in a child's developmental progress. The parent is the person who knows their child best so they must be able to share their views and be a part of the assessment process. All observations should be kept and recorded in a file or folder that the parent's have access to at any time.

POINT FOR REFLECTION

When carrying out observations do you:

- Make time to observe by involving another member of staff to cover for you while you observe?

- Decide who and what you wish to observe? Do you want to focus on a particular child, an area of development, or the use of an area within the setting.

- Decide on the method of observation you will use?

- Maintain confidentiality and keep reports clear and concise?

To be able to make child-centred observations you need to be attentive to what it is the child is actually doing and saying, what they are trying to do and say and notice what is yet beyond their capabilities. You may notice that they have a schema for a particular type of activity and so plan to provide similar activities that they will enjoy. In this way you are building up your knowledge of individual strengths and interests, which will aid you in meeting your aim of inclusive practice for all children.

It is good practice to set aside time for observation if possible throughout the day, or carry a notepad and pen around with you to jot things down that you feel are important. You also need to decide what it is you want to observe and why. Reasons for doing observations may be to look at one of the following:

- To assess the child's age and stage of development

- To evaluate any health and safety issues

- To evaluate the effectiveness of activities provided

- Physical growth and development, individual characteristics

- Communication and language development

- Cognitive skills and intellectual development and ability

- Emotional development expression of feelings and behaviour

- Social development and integration, relationships

- Styles and approaches to learning

- Evidence of independence, confidence, maturity or immaturity

- Changes in behaviour — reactions and responses to given situations

The principles of observation

The main principles for observing children are so that practitioners can:

- Make recommendations for the future from what has been observed and develop strategies to help and support the child

- Identify and resolve any problems that the child may be experiencing

Table 3: A development log at a glance

Child's name Age	Personal, Social and Emotional Development	Communication, Language and Literacy	Problem Solving, Reasoning and Numeracy	Knowledge and Understanding of the World	Physical Development	Creative Development
0-11 months						
8-20 months						
16-26 months						
22-36 months						
30-50 months						
40-60 months						

- Report to parents and other professionals for the benefit of the child

- Identify any personal or environmental factors that may influence the child's development

Development charts

Development charts are an easy way to look at the overall development of the child and see at a glance the areas of development that the child may need help and support in. The charts consist of a graph with areas of development marked along the bottom and age in months along the vertical axis. The idea is to plot the age-appropriate level of development for each child in each of the areas of learning by marking it with a cross. These are particularly good for charting the development of children with special or additional needs. See table 3 on page 49 for an example of this.

Most nurseries now have access to digital cameras and may use them to record events and special days within the setting. They can be a useful tool in observations and are good for recording developmental stages. Camcorders are fantastic for recording types of behaviour and development, and can be used when working with parents and students to help them to understand developmental stages. Permission must be sought from parents to use either of these methods of observation.

Evaluating what you have learned

Once we have gathered all of the information from our observations we must be careful about factors that influence our attitudes, including: our own belief systems; the belief systems of the child and their family; cultural differences; environmental factors; media factors; lifestyle choices of the family; and any preconceived ideas that we may have.

Look back on any observation and try to decide if the aims and purpose of doing it have been met. Does the child meet the developmental norms for their age/stage of development? What kind of activities may help support the child towards the next stage of development? Is there some underlying factor that you had not noticed before? Does it give you a clearer understanding of the child's needs? Does the child need further observation in order to assess them more accurately?

When observing children it is vital to avoid stereotyping individuals, as well as to consider whether children's actions are a one-off occurrence or usual patterns of behaviour.

POINTS FOR REFLECTION

- Look at the inclusion policy for your setting — does it give real examples of how this is put into practice?

- Think about how the staff help children with self-esteem and positive self images.

- How do you ensure you respect the individual child with regards to their cultures and beliefs? How do you demonstrate this within the setting?

- What planning do you make for raising self-esteem and praising children in the setting?

KEY POINTS IN WORKING WITH PLANNING AND RESOURCING

- Look at your learning environment: how do they reflect inclusion and diversity? Think about all stages of the children's development in these areas.

- How much heuristic play do you have in your setting? Start collecting objects to make treasure baskets or discovery boxes for learning and exploration.

- The outdoor environment is just as important as the indoor environment when considering inclusion and diversity.

- Promote positive self-esteem in order to support children's sense of self-worth and pride.

- Look at the record keeping, planning and assessment processes that are in place. Do they need changing or updating?

- Think about your own values and beliefs and how they could affect the setting and families who attend.

Chapter 6

Leadership and reflective practice

As a leader, you are pivotal in the development of inclusive practice within your setting. Others will look to you for guidance and support when addressing issues of equality and diversity.

You will not only need to model the type of practice you expect to see but you will also need to provide access to training, professional development opportunities, and other support and guidance needed or required by your team.

If you haven't discussed your values and vision with your staff team, then a good place to begin is to have that discussion. In a staff meeting or team discussion, ask people to record on a Post-it note a value that they hold dear — something that is really important to them or that they would have to challenge if they saw someone not adhering to it. Get them to share these with on another. Then undertake a sorting activity — look for key themes, repeated words, etc. This should enable you as a group to come up with a list of the values that you all hold dear. These can be used to create a quality charter for display around your setting.

An example of a quality charter

At our setting:

- Quality learning comes first

- Children, parents and staff work together

- Everyone is special and enriches the life of our setting

- Hard work and achievements are always celebrated

- We are kind to each other

- We take pride in ourselves

- We are always ready to listen

- We make all visitors welcome

Leading by example

Being an inclusive leader is more than just having your policies and systems in place. Actions speak much louder than words. As a leader you are always being observed by people with whom you work, so it is really important that you always remember this in your dealings with others. The old adage "do as I say and not as I do" is not acceptable and you must act as a good role model for everyone. You must be strong in your commitment to equality and inclusion and demonstrate this on a daily basis. You need to show respect in the way you talk to other people, welcome them to your setting and work with them.

You need to ensure that your staff have an understanding of the cultures that make up your community, it is so easy to offend through ignorance — remember to ask if you are unsure.

Remember, as mentioned in chapter one, it is not about treating everyone the same, but it is important that you treat everyone with the same level of respect.

Training

Training courses are a good way of updating knowledge and implementing new ways of doing things and there are usually several new ones each year for staff to attend which are informative and thought-provoking and help the practitioner see things differently about the setting.

Each local authority and family information service will have free courses for practitioners to attend throughout the year, and there may even be a pot of funding available to the setting to provide

The development of any practice should be securely underpinned by the values and shared vision you have for your setting. A key ingredient to the success of your work is the extent to which these values are shared by all the members of your community. Life outside may be very different, but in your setting there should be a code of conduct and of behaviour which everyone should try to sustain in their dealings with each other and the outside world.

Values need to be consistent. Everything matters, not for what you do but for the way in which it is done — the way you do it. What you are hopeful of is that the way you live your values will rub off on others around you. In that way, you will be building the ethos of your setting together.

Some questions to consider:

- What are the values that you espouse?

- How do you live those values on a day to day basis?

- Have you noticed other staff, children, or parents copying the way you do things? Have you discussed your values with your staff team?

for staff cover while key staff attend. The courses are usually linked to themes and principles of the EYFS and other issues relating to care and education. Staff should be allowed to attend courses that interest them or that they have been requesting for a while as it will help the setting and help the staff member to strive towards best practice. Staff should be encouraged to think about the type of training that they would like to access so that they can discuss this with you during supervision sessions, performance reviews or appraisal meetings. You need to ensure that all staff have access to training opportunities and support to enable them to fulfil their role and responsibilities. Keeping a training log will help you monitor the training accessed by each staff member so that you can ensure equity.

Training can be shared at staff meetings and information put forward about new ideas and ways of doing things acted on if it will suit the setting. Training helps to keep the staff motivated

and up-to-date on current best practice and may inspire them towards innovative new ways of letting children access the curriculum through small changes to the room, or by actively using new ideas to make things run more smoothly.

All training certificates should be kept in the professional development portfolio and staff should get at least two full training days a year for their own personal development. Other courses such as child protection, first aid and food hygiene should be kept up to date every three years, or when indicated by the date on each member of staff's certificate.

Reflective practice

Early years practitioners should keep a reflective journal and record their journey of achievements and progression as often as possible. If there are new tasks that need completing or areas for improvement they can be recorded in the journal and reflected on at a later date. It is helpful to gauge how well things have gone and what could have been improved and how. The journal will also help Early Years Professional Status candidates with the written tasks, as they will have a record of what happened, when, and how. It is a good idea to share this reflective journal with other practitioners so that they may give feedback and offer an alternative perspective.

Research and up-to-date knowledge

All childcare and education workers have a duty to keep themselves up to date with current policy and legislative requirements. Perhaps keep a box in the staff room of publications and booklets (marking up those that can be downloaded) that would be helpful for others to read and understand. Set up an inclusion and diversity noticeboard where interesting articles, and policies can be displayed. See pages 63-64 of this book for a list of relevant articles and books which specifically address issues surrounding inclusion and diversity.

Ensure that any government papers you have on file are up-to-date and replaced as soon as possible. If possible subscribe to a good early years magazine that informs you of the latest news on legislation and policy.

Early Years Professionals should be instrumental in modelling active researching and information sharing to inspire others,

Example: Developing staff as reflective practitioners

Keeping a reflective journal can support staff in developing their practice

In one early years setting all staff are encouraged to reflect on their practice as a means to secure continuous improvement. This is done in several ways:

- New staff are allocated into teams with more experienced staff members who can mentor and support, not just during their induction period, but throughout the period of their employment. Staff can discuss any aspects of their practice with their mentor, who will not just provide answers but will support their mentees in finding their own solutions. This practice encourages staff members to reflect on their practice, identifying what they think happened, and what they might have done differently.

- During staff or team meetings, staff are encouraged to share good practice or contribute to policy development based on their own reflections.

- Staff are encouraged to keep a reflective journal so that they can keep their own personal record of their thinking and practice. The journal is a private space where they can explore incidents, issues, and knotty problems. By writing it down the emotional engagement with the issue is made less personal and staff can return to the issue later in order to analyse what was going on in more depth. It is also a space where practitioners can jot down ideas and be creative about finding new solutions. Staff know that their journals are private and no-one will ever ask to see them, so that they can be honest about their practice. They are encouraged to review their reflective journals before performance management meetings in order to identify aspects of their work that have gone well and others where they feel they need further guidance.

- Supervision is offered to all staff,each member of staff is asked to identify areas of their work that they wish to discuss with their supervisor. Their supervisor will support them in exploring the issue, but will not offer solutions.

The benefits of developing staff as reflective practitioners are many. The senior leaders at the setting find that staff are more empowered; effective practice is more widely shared through professional discussions; policy and practice are developed with new ideas readily generated and trialled with confidence, and most importantly, outcomes for children are improved.

LINKS WITH YOUR PRACTICE

Practitioners may also find it useful to use their reflective journal to help them think through difficult situations or 'knotty problems'. They might find the following process useful as a way to think through some of these issues. The technique is called 'critical incident analysis' and it has the following components:

1. Phenomenon: describe the experience/incident/matter to investigate — exactly what happened, who said what, etc.

2. Causal: what contributed to this experience/incident/matter? Why do you think it happened?

3. Context: what are the significant background factors behind this experience/incident/matter?

4. Reflection: what was I trying to achieve? Why did I intervene as I did? What were the consequences of my actions for myself/others? How did I feel about the experience whilst it was happening? How did others feel about it? How do I know how others feel about it? What factors or knowledge influenced my decisions and actions?

5. Alternative actions: what others choices did I have? What would be the consequences of these other choices?

6. Learning: how do I feel about the experience/incident/matter? Could I have dealt better with the situation? What have I learned from this experience? What will I do or not do next time?

(Adapted from Johns, C. (1995) pp. 222-34).

By keeping a reflective journal, you will be able to track your behaviours over time. You may see a pattern emerging in the way you respond to particular people or situations or at particular times. By acknowledging these patterns in your behaviour, you will become more aware of 'trigger' situations and can modify your approach. It is by trying something different yourself that you will encourage others to be different too. You should find that you will gain confidence by knowing yourself better, which will in turn improve your relationships with others.

although some staff members may not be as interested to learn new ways of doing things. They should be encouraged to understand that nothing stands still and that changing the way we look at and do things can have many positive benefits for the children that we care for.

Visiting other settings

It is a good idea to visit other early years settings to get a different view on how other practitioners deal with situations and arrangements of their rooms to ensure that all children can access all areas. This may instigate the need for change to your own practice or inspire you to have new ideas of your own.

Sharing good practice should be a positive part of the learning community you are trying to foster, and not something that practitioners feel threatened by. It is flattering if somebody else likes your work and wishes to adapt your ideas to suit their own needs and requirements, likewise they may have ideas that you can use.

Selecting staff

Selecting staff becomes quite important when considering inclusion and diversity.

Staff meetings are ideal for sharing information

LINKS WITH YOUR PRACTICE

Encourage staff to undertake their own mini-research projects — it is simply a matter of choosing an area that they find interesting and noticing things about that particular aspect of practice. It would be more beneficial if they recorded their 'noticings' either in a learning journal or even on sticky notes and then they could discuss their findings with colleagues. This simple practice can often lead practitioners to question the way we do things around here and come up with new and exciting ways of improving practice.

Outcomes of these mini-research projects could be shared during team meetings and other practitioners could be encouraged to question or discuss the findings together. Another idea is to have one wall in the staffroom dedicated to research. Staff could be encouraged to pin up articles they have found interesting, photographs of their research with some interesting questions for others to consider, etc.

One way of modelling to your community that you respect the diversity of cultures is to include in your staff team people from a range of ethnic backgrounds. Having staff who can speak community languages will also help with communication with parents for whom English is not their first language. It will show that you have a real commitment to meeting community needs and it will make parents feel more confident about approaching your setting for advice and support.

Another aspect to consider is the gender profile of your workforce. Early years work is predominantly a female domain. This can mean that children do not have access to a male role model in your setting, which could lead them to think that working with young children is women's work — thereby reinforcing a stereotype.

There are also legal requirements in terms of recruitment and selection of staff of which you need to be mindful — see the section on equality policy in chapter three.

Recruitment and selection policy

It is best practice to have a recruitment and selection policy in place — your local authority's human resources department will probably be able to provide you with some guidance on this. But as a minimum, you should explain to prospective applicants why you are asking for particular pieces of information, e.g. asking for the date of birth of applicants because it is necessary to ensure that you comply with the safer recruitment obligations by undertaking due diligence on career history.

When a vacancy occurs

The job description and person specification should be drawn up to focus on the duties and the qualifications required. It should include:

- The job title (which must be sex and age neutral)

- The location of the job

- Grade of the post

- The person to whom the postholder is responsible

- Any people reporting to the postholder

- Main purpose of the job

- Main duties and responsibilities

- Any special working conditions (e.g. shift or working patterns, the requirement for a criminal record check)

The language used in the job description should:

- Avoid jargon and unexplained acronyms and abbreviations

- Be easily understandable to potential applicants for the post

- Use inclusive, non-discriminatory language

The person specification is of equal importance to the job description and it should be used to inform the selection of people for interview. It should detail the skills, experience, abilities and expertise that are required to do the job, stating which are essential and which are desirable, and should be used to inform the contents of the advertisement. It should be specific, related to the job and should not include any criteria that could be thought of as discriminatory under the Equality Act 2010.

Monitoring and evaluation

An important aspect of your leadership work in terms of leading inclusive practice is the monitoring and evaluation that you undertake. It is the way that you truly find out what is happening in your setting and provides you with evidence on which to base your judgements about the effectiveness of your policy, procedures and practice in terms of meeting the requirements of inclusive practice. It is a way of you finding out if you do what you say you do — just because something is written in a policy document, doesn't mean that it is fully understood and implemented consistently across your setting.

It is also a way of demonstrating to Ofsted that you are a setting that is capable of accurate self-evaluation and that you have the capacity to improve.

Getting ready for inspection

We have considered the legal aspects of Ofsted inspections in chapter three. We are now going to look at how to prepare yourself for an Ofsted inspection as a setting. What do you need to do to ensure that you, your staff, your governors or management board and families are all as fully prepared for inspection as they can be? How can you demonstrate that your setting celebrates inclusion and diversity?

Firstly, it is important that you ensure that your self-evaluation form (SEF) is up-to-date, because this is what the inspectors will use to prepare for your inspection. See the table on page 22 to aid you in your SEF preparation.

Your lead inspector will use your self-evaluation form to identify the focus for inspection and to plan inspection activities. Your self-evaluation should show how you have reached conclusions about your effectiveness, and the improvements that you have made since your last evaluation. It should include or signpost the reader to the needs analysis, data, case studies, evaluations and other assessments it makes to support its conclusions. Remember you need to demonstrate the impact of your services. Try to make sure that you have a wide range of examples of inclusion and celebrations of diversity within your evidence collection. Inspectors test the accuracy of self-evaluation at inspection when coming to judgements about leadership, management and overall effectiveness.

Ofsted inspections will look at how centres:

- Help children and families in their reach area access early childhood services and show them the benefit of doing so. Are you reaching a wide cross-section of your population or are there particular groups who are not accessing services?

- Improve outcomes for young children. Are you narrowing the achievement gap?

You will also need to give due consideration to the services and activities available during the days of inspection, including any off-site activities, and to arrange interviews with key people you wish the inspector to talk to such as health professionals, training delivery partners, childcare managers, childminder network coordinators and so on. By involving a wide range of partners you are demonstrating the inclusive nature of your provision. You might also want to invite the local authority lead officer to be involved in the inspection.

POINT FOR REFLECTION

You need to ensure when selecting staff that you are inclusive in your recruitment and selection processes, and that you select all employees in an equitable, effective, and efficient manner to ensure the provision of the most effective personnel to meet your requirements.

The recruitment and selection procedure should enable you to attract applicants from diverse backgrounds and ensure that recruitment is carried out without discrimination on the grounds of race, ethnicity, nationality, national origin, colour, disability, age, religion or belief, sexual orientation or any other unjustifiable criterion.

You need to consider your recruitment process and ensure that at each stage you minimise the risk of the possibility of discrimination.

Some questions to consider:

- Does your current staff profile reflect the community it serves in terms of ethnicity and languages spoken?

- Do the children see good male role models as part of your staff team?

So what is it that Ofsted looks for on inspection?

- Centres must be able to demonstrate how they have identified and selected the services they must offer and those they choose to offer for children and their families, based on their knowledge of the local area and the targets for improvement within that local area (rather than targets for the wider local authority area). You will want to demonstrate that you have accurate knowledge and information about the diversity of your locality. This includes how they have consulted effectively with users (and potential users) to establish their needs, demonstrating that you are inclusive of parents' views and ideas. Users should also be represented on the centre's parent forum and the centre's advisory board. Inspectors will look for evidence that user's views have shaped services.

- Centres must also demonstrate that they are improving outcomes — evaluation of their services to show this is critical.

- Partnership working is essential in children's centres. Services must be coordinated and integrated and Ofsted look for evidence of the centre's and the local authority's efforts to make this happen. You will want to demonstrate that you have engaged the correct services and agencies to meet the diverse needs of your local population.

- The policies and procedures for safeguarding and child protection must be clear, explicit and understood by all.

- Leaders and managers must demonstrate how well they know the community and how the centres services and activities meet its needs.

The inspection activities on site are very much like all Ofsted inspections. They concentrate on evidence gathering through observations, interviews, and scrutiny of information, talking to key partners and stakeholders — make sure that you present a wide range of people to interview, making sure that you have representatives from main community groups and specific groups, such as dads or young parents. Ofsted does not intend to see all the services on offer or judge the quality of each and every individual service. Inspectors are more interested in whether the activities on offer are the right activities, how the centre knows that they are the right ones and whether the centre knows if they are making a difference. This is where the time spent on self-evaluation and monitoring of services will pay dividends. You should be keeping

monitoring records of attendance at groups and sessions, ensuring that you have collected ethnicity data from parents on registration. In this way you can produce accurate reports for the Ofsted team on which ethnic groups are accessing which services. You will also need to demonstrate how you are trying to reach the most vulnerable groups in your locality, so this will need careful consideration.

Inspections will focus on an evaluation of how well the centre is improving outcomes for all of the children and families it serves.

When making judgements on the quality of provision, inspectors take account of:

- How effectively the centre ensures that users' health and social needs are appropriately assessed.

- How well the centre works in partnership with other agencies to ensure that assessments, such as those carried out under the Common Assessment Framework and assessments of children with learning difficulties and/or disabilities are robust and well-informed.

Where adult and community learning is offered:

- Whether programmes of work are negotiated with adult learners to accurately reflect their abilities and aspirations.

- Whether adult learners' achievements and learning goals are recorded and accredited.

- To what extent assessment information about individual and diverse groups of learners is used in programme and course development.

Inspections consider the quality of outreach: how well the centre does this; how this helps to reduce the sense of isolation for some families; and how it helps to build independence for families rather than dependence. Centres need to show how they help families move on, rather than have them coming back for the same things time and again.

Centres do need to consider the balance of universal services for all children in the community and targeted services for those families and children in most need. There needs to be a balance between what is offered so that centres are not seen as preventing some families accessing services — whether these are families who are less in need or those that are most in need.

Ofsted grades

Inspectors always use their professional judgement when weighing up the evidence to determine the grades to be awarded. However, the judgements on safeguarding and equality and diversity are significant. Where a judgement of inadequate is awarded for safeguarding or equality and diversity it is unlikely that the leadership and management judgement will be better than satisfactory and it is most likely to be inadequate.

Equality and diversity focuses on how effectively the centre is narrowing the achievement gap and how effectively the centre actively promotes equality and diversity and tackles discrimination. Inspectors will look at whether the centre is doing all it can to make sure families are able to access to early childhood services. Failure to engage with a particular section of the community will have a significant impact on a number of judgements, including overall effectiveness.

Safeguarding practice and guidance is underpinned by a duty for children's centres to cooperate with relevant agencies to safeguard and promote the welfare of children and vulnerable adults. The protection of children is of the highest priority for Ofsted across all its inspection remits. The staying safe judgement will influence the safeguarding judgement.

Inspectors expect to see that efforts to reach those most difficult or unwilling to engage are targeted and that outreach is proving effective in encouraging wider access to services.

Inspectors will make their judgments based on the following framework.

How good are outcomes for users?

- The extent to which children, including those from vulnerable groups, are physically, mentally and emotionally healthy and families have healthy lifestyles.

- The extent to which children are safe and protected, their welfare concerns are identified and appropriate steps taken to address them.

- The extent to which all users enjoy and achieve educationally and in their personal and social development.

- The extent to which children engage in positive behavior and develop positive relationships and users contribute to decision-making and governance of the centre.

LINKS WITH YOUR PRACTICE

Here are some questions that Ofsted may well ask of settings:

- Are we sure we have identified all potential users including any groups or individuals that may find it more difficult to access services?

- How do we know what we are providing is right for this area?

- Are the right users coming into the centre and if not what are we doing about it?

- What are the success criteria for the services we provide — are we setting ourselves challenging but realistic targets, and measuring whether we meet these?

- Are we involving everyone, including users and other agencies, in evaluating our impact

- What data and evidence do we have or need to start to collect to support our evaluation of services?

- The extent to which children are developing skills for the future and parents are developing economic stability and independence.

How good is the provision?

- The effectiveness of the assessment of the needs of children, parents and other users.

- The extent to which the centre promotes purposeful learning, development and enjoyment for all users.

- The extent to which the range of services, activities and opportunities meet the needs of users and the wider community.

- The quality of guidance, care, and support offered to users within the centre and the wider community.

How effective are the leadership and management?

- The extent to which governance, accountability, professional supervision and day-to-day management arrangements are clear and understood.

- The extent to which ambitious targets drive improvement, provision is integrated, and there are high expectations for users and the wider community.

- The extent to which resources are used and managed efficiently and effectively to meet the needs of users and the wider community.

- The extent to which equality is promoted and diversity celebrated, illegal or unlawful discrimination is tackled and the centre fulfils its statutory duties.

- The effectiveness of the centre's policy, procedures and work with key agencies in safeguarding children and, where applicable, vulnerable adults.

- The extent to which evaluation is used to shape and improve services and activities.

- The extent to which partnerships with other agencies ensure the integrated delivery of the range of services the centre has been commissioned to provide.

- The extent to which the centre supports and encourages the wider community to engage with services and uses their views to develop the range of provision.

Differences in inspection arrangements in Scotland, Wales and Northern Ireland

Scotland

In Scotland, settings will be inspected by the HM Inspectorate of Education (HMIE), which is an executive agency of the Scottish Government. HMIE inspect settings approximately every seven years, or more often when there are reasons to do so. There will usually only be one inspector. In large settings, the team will include a second team member who may be a Social Care and Social Work Improvement Scotland (SCSWIS) officer. SCSWIS inspects pre-school and nursery classes every two years, or every year if there are children younger than three years.

The inspection report will highlight what the setting does well and where it needs to improve. It will answer the following questions:

- How well do children learn and achieve?

- Does the setting have a clear sense of direction?

- How well do staff work with others to support children's learning?

- Are staff and children actively involved in their community?

- Does the setting have high expectations of all children?

For more information see <www.hmie.gov.uk> or <www.scswis.com>.

Wales

Estyn is the office of Her Majesty's Chief Inspector of Education and Training in Wales. The inspection team will be led by a reporting inspector. Most inspections will be led by HMI. Each inspection team includes a lay inspector and a peer inspector (current teachers or managers from another setting). Each setting can have someone who works there on the inspection team. This nominee keeps the inspectors informed about the setting and its work.

Settings are inspected every six years and will generally receive about four weeks' notice of their inspection. All inspections start with the setting's evaluation of their own work and data about its performance.

The report will include:

- An overall judgment on current performance

- An overall judgment on the setting's prospects for improvement

It will also have judgments on:

- Outcomes — the standards achieved by children and their wellbeing

- Provision — learning experiences, teaching, care, support and guidance, and the learning environment

Leadership and reflective practice

- Leadership — leadership, improving quality, partnership working and resource management

All judgments are based on a four-point scale: excellent, good, adequate or unsatisfactory.

For more information see <www.estyn.gov.uk>.

Northern Ireland

Inspections are undertaken by The Education and Training Inspectorate (ETI). There are three different types of inspection: type A, B or C.

Type A and Type C inspections are carried out by two inspectors, or an inspector accompanied by an associate assessor. Type B inspections are carried out by one inspector or in the case of a large nursery unit, one inspector plus an associate assessor.

The inspectors will give most emphasis to the quality of children's development and learning and how well these are promoted in all aspects of the pre-school curriculum set out in the *Curricular Guidance for Pre-School Education*. They will consider a range of factors which affect the quality of the children's development and learning and will make judgments on their effectiveness.

These factors will include:

- The ethos of the centre

- The quality of the staff's work with the children

- The organisation of the curriculum

- The provision for children with special educational needs

- The centre's relationships with parents

- Planning, assessment, recording and reporting

- Leadership and management, including development planning and self-evaluation

- Staffing and staff development, including training and qualifications

- Links with schools and other agencies

- Healthy eating and physical activity

- Accommodation and resources

For more information see <www.etini.gov.uk>.

KEY POINTS IN WORKING WITH LEADERSHIP AND REFLECTIVE PRACTICE

- As a leader, you set the tone for your setting. You need to lead by example and be an exemplary role model for children, parents and staff.

- All staff should be encouraged to develop as reflective practitioners. By evaluating their practice and considering how it could be improved to meet the individual needs of the children in their care, they will be contributing to the raising of standards and the development of inclusive practice in your setting.

- Training and research will contribute to the development of practice. Staff should be encouraged to know their own learning needs.

- Selecting staff is an important aspect of the leader's work. You will need to consider the profile of your staff group to ensure that you have the staff to enable you to meet the diverse needs of your local community.

- Monitoring and evaluation are crucial if you are to secure continuous improvement. Consider who undertakes the monitoring, how it is done and what happens to the information collected. Any monitoring and evaluation needs to feed into future planning and changes for improvements in practice.

- Inspection should not be seen as a one-off event. All your work should be leading up to presenting your setting in its best light. You should demonstrate that you can make an honest appraisal of your setting's strengths and you know which areas require further development. It will also be in your favour if you have considered how you will address areas which require development.

Glossary of terms

One of the issues in developing inclusion and respecting diversity is the language we use to describe it. There is a plethora of language around inclusion and diversity and it is all too easy to offend people by using language inappropriately or by not truly understanding the meaning of the word in its context.

African Caribbean: people from the Caribbean whose heritage is African

Anti-discriminatory: policies, practices and procedures that acknowledge that discrimination exists, giving consideration to appropriate actions that need to be taken to remove it

Asian: people from, or whose family originates from Asia

Assumptions: a supposition that traits or characteristics are generalised across all people from a particular group

Black: people from an African or Afro-Caribbean background

Class: a social rank based on aspects of people's lives, e.g. education, background, occupation, lifestyle, wealth

Culture: factors that have contributed to people's lives and experiences, e.g. language, social class, religious beliefs and practices, traditions, dress and food

Discrimination: when someone is treated less favourably than others because of certain characteristics they possess. This can be direct, indirect, or institutionalised

Disability: a physical or mental condition that has a long-term adverse effect on the individual's capacity to live a 'normal' life

Diversity: differences, distinctiveness

Equality: treating people as individuals, according to their specific needs

Ethnicity: an individual's cultural, national or religious identity

Ethnic minority: a group within a community which has different national or cultural traditions from the main population

Gay: a person who is sexually attracted to the same sex

Gender/sex: either of the two main categories (male and female) into which humans are divided on the basis of their reproductive functions

Harassment: verbal, non-verbal or physical aggression towards people who are different

Inclusion: a process of identifying, understanding and breaking down barriers to participation and belonging (devised by the National Early Childhood Forum in 2003)

Integration: the intermixing of people who were previously segregated

Mainstreaming: bringing a child with special educational needs into a school or class for pupils who do not have special needs

Mixed race: denoting or relating to people whose parents or ancestors are from different ethnic backgrounds

Multiculturalism: relating to or containing several cultural or ethnic groups within a society

Non-white: denoting or relating to a person whose origin is not predominantly European

Positive action/positive discrimination: the practice or policy of favouring individuals belonging to groups which suffer discrimination

Glossary ot terms

Prejudice: preconceived opinion that is not based on reason or actual experience/dislike, hostility, or unjust behaviour deriving from preconceived and unfounded opinions

Race: the fact or condition of belonging to a racial division or group; the qualities or characteristics associated with this/a group of people sharing the same culture, history, language, etc.; an ethnic group

Racism: prejudice, discrimination, or antagonism directed against someone of a different race based on the belief that one's own race is superior

Sexism: prejudice, stereotyping, or discrimination, typically against women, on the basis of sex

Sexual orientation: a person's sexual identity in relation to the gender to which they are attracted; the fact of being heterosexual, homosexual, or bisexual

South Asian: people from, or whose family originates from India, Bangladesh, Pakistan and Sri Lanka

Special educational needs (SEN): children who have a developmental delay, a disability or health problem, a speech or language disorder, emotional and/or behavioural difficulties or a learning difficulty such as dyslexia are deemed to have special educational needs

Stereotyping: a widely held but fixed and oversimplified image or idea of a particular type of person or thing

Travellers, Roma and Gypsies and other travelling communities: members of nomadic populations

White: belonging to or denoting a human group having light-coloured skin (chiefly used of people of European extraction)

Books and websites

Booth, T., Ainscow, M. (2000) *Index for inclusion. Developing learning and participation in schools*. Bristol: Centre for Studies on Inclusive Education (CSIE).

CRE (2000) *Learning for All: Standards for Racial Equality*. London: Commission for Racial Equality.

Department for Children, Schools and Families (2008) *Statutory Framework for the Early Years Foundation Stage: Setting the standards for learning, development and care for children from birth to five*. Nottingham: DCSF.

Department for Children, Schools and Families (2008), *The Impact of Parental Involvement on Children's Education*. Nottingham: DCSF.

Department for Education and Science (1985) *Education for All: The Swann Report*. London: HMSO.

Department for Education and Skills (DfES) (2001) *Inclusive Schooling: Children with Special Educational Needs*. London: DfES.

DfES (2001) *SEN Code of Practice*. Nottingham: DfES.

Early Childhood Forum (2003) *Participation and Belonging in Early Years Settings*. National Children's Bureau. [Internet]. Available from: <http://www.ncb.org.uk/dotpdf/open%20 access%20-%20phase%201%20only/leaflet_ecf.pdf>.

Education Act 1981. London: HMSO.

Education Act 1996. London: HMSO.

Ellis, R. (1999) *Learning a Second Language Through Interaction*. Amsterdam: John Benjamin.

Evangelou, M., Sylva, K. (2003) *The Effects of the Peers Early Educational Partnership (PEEP) on Children's Developmental Progress*. Nottingham: DfES.

Goldschmied, E., Jackson, S. (2004) *People Under Three, Young Children in Day Care*. (2nd edition) London: Routledge.

Greenfield, S. (2001) *The Private Life of the Brain*. London: Penguin Books.

Jensen, E. (1994) *The Learning Brain*. San Diego: Brain Store.

Johns, C. (1995) Framing Learning Through Reflection Within Carper's Fundamental Ways of Knowing in Nursing. *Journal of Advanced Nursing*. 22, pp. 222-234.

Ofsted (2009) *Early Years Online Self-Evaluation Form (SEF) and Guidance for Settings Delivering the Early Years Foundation Stage*. London: Ofsted.

Qualifications and Curriculum Authority (2000) *Curriculum Guidance for the Foundation Stage*. London: QCA.

UN General Assembly (1989) *Convention on the Rights of the Child*. Treaty Series, United Nations, vol. 1577, p. 3. [Internet]. Available from: <http://www.unhcr.org/refworld/docid/3ae6b38f0.html>.

Warnock Committee (1978) *Special Educational Needs: the Warnock Report*. London: DES.

Additional sources of information

Centre for Studies on Inclusive Education (CSIE)
Coldharbour Lane, Frenchay, Bristol, BS16 1QU
Tel: 0117 328 4007
www.inclusion.org.uk

Commission for Equality and Human Rights
www.equalityhumanrights.com

Department for Education
www.education.gov.uk

DirectGov
www.direct.gov.uk

Home Office
www.homeoffice.gov.uk

National Association of Special Educational Needs
4/5 Amber Business Village, Amker Close, Tamworth, B77 4RP
Tel: 0182 7311 500
www.nasen.org.uk

National Parent Partnership Network
8 Wakely Street, London, EC1V 7QE
Tel: 020 7843 6058
www.parentpartnership.org.uk

Network 81
1-7 Woodfield Terrace, Stansted, Essex, CM24 8AJ
0845 077 4055
www.network81.org

Parents for Inclusion
Unit 2, 70 South Lambeth Road, London, SW8 1RL
Tel: 020 7735 7735
Getting A Life Help Line: 020 7582 5008
www.parentsforinclusion.org

Pre-School Learning Alliance
69 Kings Cross Road, London, WC1X 9LL
Tel: 020 7833 0991
E-mail: pla@pre-school.org.uk
Website: www.pre-school.org.uk

Stonewall: Equality and Justice for Lesbians, Gay Men and Bisexuals
www.stonewall.org.uk

Sure Start
www.surestart.gov.uk

The Alliance for Inclusive Education
366 Brixton Road, London, SW9 7AA
020 7737 6030
www.inclusion.org.uk

The Children's National Service Framework
www.dh.gov.uk